Man in a Puddle

The Nightmare, Canepatch and Ten Thousand Islands

MARK RUTKOWSKI

While I was editing this story, the whistling winds of Hurricane Irma were just beginning to batter my inadequate oceanfront windows. The eye of the storm was expected to make landfall somewhere on the southwest tip of Florida. The settings where this story takes place; Cape Sable, Whitewater Bay, The Nightmare, Shark River and the Thompson Homestead, were about to endure sustained winds of one hundred-thirty mph and gusts much higher. All that combined with a storm surge of eight feet.

Those details speak for themselves.

A few days before the storm's arrival, I was walking on the beach headed to the supermarket to stock up when I got the call that my father had passed away in hospice that morning. It was not unexpected but a shock just the same. Memories flooded my mind as I tried to stay focused on the crisis at hand. The Chinese saying *"may you live in interesting times"* came to mind.

By Saturday night I was alternating between mopping up a small amount of water coming through the cracks in the windows and door to calling friends to watching the moving pinwheel image repeating on the weather channel.

Then the first feeder bands arrived spawning tornadoes and my internet and cable connection came to an abrupt end.

At daylight, the storm would arrive in earnest. I was already exhausted so I took a nap on the couch. The power went out sometime while I slept.

I woke up at six to the sound of rattling windows and screaming wind. I leapt off the couch. My feet splashed in a puddle an inch deep.

Out of my mouth the words formed that would be my mantra for the next twelve hours, *"Fight the storm, fight the storm!"*

From six until ten, rain sprayed, squirted and poured in through every crack in the wall and windows including the electrical outlets. I ran from room to room fortifying the boarded-up windows while mopping and sponging like a madman. I shoved all the rags and towels I could to find into the gaps and twisted them to a point to wick the water into buckets. Meanwhile the storm grew louder and louder, screaming like a banshee and pounding the windows like a giant boxing glove.

Since Irma was so big, the break I expected from the rotation never came. I was forced to fight the storm relentlessly as it blew from the northeast for 3.5 hours, then from the east for 3.5 hours and then from the southeast for 3.5 hours. Almost twelve hours of the worst, most testing, steady winds from what is known as the "dirty side" of the hurricane.

I couldn't stop bailing. It was as if my home had been thrown into the sea. Each time I said *"it can't get any worse"*, Irma found a way to get worse. I stopped saying it. At high tide the sea washed over the dunes and flushed onto Collins Avenue. The wind speed increased and the pitch of the banshee scream rose to the point where the even the slightest modulation made you jump.

I ran from room to room, emptying buckets, wringing out soaked towels, moping and sponging the floor next to windows that threatened to break at any moment. I had to stay ahead of it.

I had to forget the future. The storm never showed a hint of letting up. If I comforted myself by thinking the storm would pass in three hours (like Wilma did), that deadline would come and go without a change. I could only tell myself it would get better in *twelve hours*, it couldn't last more than twelve hours!

Somewhere in the battle, my mind fell silent. Thinking dissipated, I fell back on my Zen training. I gave up. I disappeared into the process, into the noise, into the danger, into the loss. I did one thing after the other over and over and left analysis behind. I disappeared into the hurricane.

And then it got worse. While taking one of the few photos of the mad sea, I heard the distinct "ping" of glass splitting. Somewhere something gave way. I bolted for my safe room. I shut the two heavy Balinese teak doors on either side of the hallway then got inside the bathroom and shut that door as well.

At any moment I expected the hurricane to violently enter my home. Maybe the war had been lost. I dropped my sponge and stood surrounded by the screaming maelstrom thinking of retreat. It may be time to collect a few things and attempt to open the hallway door (dangerously changing the pressure), and retreat to the *city of refuge*, the storage room in the center of the building.

I waited for a sign.

But the windows held, my nerves settled and I got back to the job. I disappeared into the practice and bailed out fifty more buckets of hurricane water until my sponges were useless shreds, the mop broke off its handle and my hands and knees were bruised and blistered. (Later I learned my neighbor's window latch had snapped during the storm. It apparently shot out with such force that it put a dent into the far wall.)

From 6 AM until 4:30 in the afternoon I fought the storm without more than a few minutes break.

When the winds finally moved SW parallel to the building (now at 130 mph), the banshee scream segued to the freight train bellow of a tornado. I tried the door to the hallway. Emergency lights reflected on a pond three inches deep and forty feet long. This was happening on the ninth floor.

Irma was the size of Ohio and it battered, blew and kicked for 24 hours. By attrition it wore down walls, glass, plywood and me. Imagine being in an F2 tornado -for a day.

Everyone's hurricane is different. Had the impact windows recently approved by the condominium been installed, my story might not have been worth mentioning.

But in the western Everglades where the Gulf rose over eight feet, conditions were exponentially worse. Days later, I received pictures of Chokoloskee and Everglades City neck deep in brown, churning seawater. My first reaction was that the photographs were inaccurate. They were images of silence. They did not record the sound and shaking of the tornado winds or the banshee scream.

In my imagination I traveled to some of the camps on the Wilderness Waterway. I went to Harney Creek chickee and watched it bend and shake in the 165 MPH winds, I held onto a post for 14-24 hours trying to hold on. I went to the entrance of The Nightmare and watched a bellowing gust rip the trees, surrealistically lift them into the sky and tail whip them out of sight. And I sat in the middle of Canepatch in Zen silence as tornadoes dropped from the sky like carousel horses across the horizon and the sea flooded the campsite to a depth of eight feet.

These were imaginary images, but only in the sense that I wasn't there. If I were, I'm sure it would have been quite a show and I might have learned a thing or two about how to survive it.

The most common phrase uttered after a hurricane is, "I wouldn't want to do that again." But then the sun comes out, the ocean calms and we stay and do it again next year.

The landscape of Florida has been formed by hurricane. It is part of the natural system that has sculpted the forests, pools and rivers of the peninsula for ages. And as is nature's way it makes its changes in violent outbursts. Silent and serene for a long time, then something comes along and in a split second rips it all to hell.

My story takes place in the sub tropic winter of 2000. I had returned from a year overseas that changed me so much that I felt lost in own home. This journey in the Everglades was an attempt to recover that home. Recover the sense of being, the sense of standing on the Earth knowing who you are, where you have been and happy in knowing that where you are at that moment is exactly where you're supposed to be.

My connection with the land and the super human forces that sculpt it helped to form the metaphor that our sense of self is constantly moved by forces far larger our selves. And in spite of our yearning for stability, who we think we are remains in constant flow and flux.

This book is dedicated to my Father.

Man in a Puddle

"On the eve of the journey, Amundsen's crew overhauled, rechecked and restowed all their gear. While on the other side of Antarctica, Scott's team celebrated the Queen's birthday with a scotch."

I studied the grainy black and white photographs, Amundsen's team and Scott's. Only one was successful in reaching the South Pole first and returning. The other in the photo seen toasting the queen didn't survive.

I set down my midnight sandwich and unstrapped both hatches of the kayak. I reopened all the dry bags and poured the contents onto the floor as if I were starting a jigsaw puzzle.

The bright lights blazed in the living room as I reviewed my checklist. It was three-pages long. Not the kind of checklist that's easy to look at. I could rely on very little on this journey. To begin with I had to bring all my water. I would be paddling through salt or brackish water the entire time. I couldn't use a purifier.

At this point in my preparation I arrived at a state of confusion. Even after many trips and expeditions, even with a fairly comprehensive list of gear from other trips, at some point I felt I was doing things haphazardly.

To help assuage my brain fog, I imagined what my day would be like in the swamp.

Wake up (alarm clock, timer?), boil water for coffee, tea or oatmeal, breakfast cold and hot,(bowls, spoon, fork, knife?), clean up (soap/sponge?).

Preparing the kayak, maps, sunblock, flip-flops, thermos, stowing the camera gear and meditation bells in the waterproof Pelican case, strapping it to the top of the kayak, making it fast. My waterproof maps under the seat pad. Paddling: sun, waves, cold, hot, on and on. In the end, the only thing I added was a second can opener. Redundancy was good planning I told myself. And along with my favorite wood paddles, I had not one but two reserve sets of aluminum paddles.

I had just concluded a year as an artist in residence at a gallery in Bali and my return had left me hollow. Indonesia was my first experience with such a different environment and culture. A culture and environment I mysteriously felt completely at home in.

I walked around the streets of Miami Beach as if a stranger. The street scenes I had painted for twenty years were now like long abandoned toys on a child's cake. So much had changed inside me. Not knowing where I stood, I became uncertain about every little decision. I doubted my inner compass. I needed to find the way back into this world. I needed to find my way back home (where was my home? What was home?).

I had just finished a ten-day Zen retreat. It was not my first.

If you get lost in the wilderness the first instruction is to stop. Wandering can only make things worse. I needed to stop, sit down where I was and take stock of what I knew and meditation was perfect for that. Here was a practice of sitting with what is, in heightened observation, a practice where one becomes *"at home with each and every thing".*

As soon as I sat on a cushion, folded my legs together and felt the ground solid below me, I heard a voice somewhere deep down say; 'Welcome home'. My meditation classes felt more like a reunion than an introduction. I found myself asking *'Have I done this before?'*

*

As I drove to the west coast of the Everglades, frivolous questions filled my mind. 'Will the Park's office hours end at noon today?' 'Will an Outward Bound group of fifty canoes be taking the trip at the same time as mine?' "Do I have my paddles?' 'Did I tie down the kayak well enough?' 'Do I have my paddles?' These questions were like gremlins in my head. I went through the pre dawn hours of loading and driving but the day was like a slowly tightening rope. I wished I had someone with me, but there was no one who had the time and I knew I would have decided to go alone anyway. Slowly the tightening rope released as I crossed the Big Cypress swamp on the old road.

In Everglades City I contacted the team I hired to drive my truck to the park town of Flamingo 100 miles south. They would leave it parked at the marina where I would arrive in February. I met with the park officer and secured the registration for each lonely camp along the stringy, meandering route. This registering was more for the search if my keys still hung at the dockmaster's office days after I was expected. With location's called *Lostman's Six, The Nightmare* and *Hell's Bay* this was a real concern. Back in the day, residents of the swamp paddled up on an abandoned flats boat carefully as sometimes it meant finding the desiccated body of a neighbor lying in it.

It was easy to get lost in the Everglades. For the entire trip I would be paddle through a string of ponds, bays, rivers and creeks as well as mangrove trails that looked much like a garden maze, but worse, there was no guarantee of a way out. Even young mangroves may not grow high but they obscured the overview of a seated kayaker. What's more the way in and out of a creek, pond or mangrove was rarely a straight line. It was a twisted noodle, a labyrinth. Back this way, around that way and you're likely to end up in the same place where you started with no idea how it happened. A GPS only showed you where you were, not the way through the maze, they were useless.

The way to get through the mangroves was:

A. Have a very accurate map.

B. Follow it without detour.

C. Confirm every landmark on the map and label them as you go.

D. Don't lose track. Go back as soon as things don't match the map. One patch of mangrove looks very much like any other patch, you're unlikely to discover where you are by paddling a little further, which is often the fatal mistake).

The fact that I was going alone had its advantages. In my opinion, two lost people are far worse than being lost alone. Even if one person has a pretty good hunch where they are, doubt from the other can be infectious and muddle the correct hunch. Tricky stuff was doubt. And doubt was not helping with this juncture of my life, wondering who I was and where I was going was just adding to the confusion.

Notes from the sketchbook 1/26/2000

The primary mood of the day has been that of introspection and anxiety, not at all like other trips [because] the necessity to carry all the drinking water (as there is none along the way) has colored the preparations with added power and sanctity. The water is holy, but if the water is holy, then why not the food? I would die without it. And the boat? What about the air? Every breath? [sic]

My notes from this period reflected my newly discovered Zen practice and its literature riddled with whimsical contradictions. In my Zen honeymoon, I embraced this contrarian speech with great enthusiasm. It was a novice's condition, this infatuation. One of the old masters called it 'the stink of Zen' and another likened it to the master pointing towards Zen and the student staring not at what was being pointed to but at his pointing finger and declaring, *"AH! Now I understand Zen!"*

*

Days were short in January and could be cold even on the southern tip of Florida. I took a room in a motel close to my launch site. There were only two motels in

Chokoloskee and both had the red neon vacancy sign on. I picked a room that had a view of the kayak launch site, a gravely patch of ground between two tall mangroves. I dragged the kayak inside the room to be with me, it was now a member of the crew.

It was early evening so I walked over to the local restaurant and ordered the frog leg/alligator tip plate special.

"Going out on the water, stranger?" the heavyset waitress asked as if we were in a scene from *Gunsmoke.*

"Yes, actually, kayaking the Wilderness Waterway, I begin tomorrow."

"Oh, bring an extra hat, its gonna be cold," she said, "more coffee?"

I was only half listening. I was ogling the black and white antique photos of Chockoloskee on the wall. They looked authentic. It was a common subject material for me, and making drawings and watercolors from these photos could have kept me busy for months.

As I walked back to the motel the sun was already low in the winter sky. Most people were settling down with a good book or a beer and an outboard engine that needed fixing. They might even be going to bed in an hour or two. But for me the energy in the room was electric, that rope of anxiety returned and tightened. I was in the last few hours of preparation.

Though I tried, I don't remember sleeping at all that night. I gave up at 4 AM, turned on the lights and started filling my water jugs. Thirteen gallons: one gallon a day plus two for unexpected reasons. Redundancy may be what saves you in a fix.

My waitress was right, the morning was cold, not just Florida cold. Real cold. The motel thermometer read 37 F. I stumbled around the brightly lit room overwhelmed. I had no sense of what to do first. I walked outside and stared at the truck. I could see my breath. I thought it was the lack of sleep that made my brain feel like a feverish, fuzzy cotton ball and that made everything blurry. But no, it was fog that covered the landscape and the bay. I walked back inside but left the motel room door open letting the cold air pour in. I worried if I shut it, I would weaken and crawl back under the covers.

It took forty minutes, more than it should have, but eventually I had everything in the truck, I took a final calm look around the room. Under the bed I found a flashlight that wasn't mine.

The launch site, the basic gravel and sand beach between mangroves, was still dark. In the east, a bruise of blue-gray light, a colorless light, hinted the start of the day though the temperature showed no hint of rising. I was getting concerned about my choice, my cold feet. I freed the kayak from the pile of gear (*how the hell is all this gonna fit in there?*) and pulled it off the truck. Bang! Boom! The empty kayak reported like a bass drum. I must have roused the entire town. I unstrapped the bulkhead covers and began sliding cans of food into the side of the hull around where I sat.

I could hear the drive-away car coming down Main Street. It was the only car on the road. The headlights made a cottony, yellow glow in the fog. The blue pick-up truck came alongside and the 20 something boy I only knew from the phone call arrangements got out and took my keys. While I unloaded he dutifully went through his own checklist that I had topped off the tank and that all the taillights worked. His girlfriend stared at me the through closed windows of the truck. I just stood blankly watching as he got his coffee and a backpack and repeated some instructions to the girl.

"Everything out of your truck?" the boy asked.

"I think so,"

"Well, check, you'd be surprised..." he said.

I walked around opening the doors peeing under the seats and opening the glovebox. I found a rope that might be handy later and tossed it on the mountain of gear surrounding the kayak.

"Good luck, your keys will be with the harbormaster at Flamingo, got it?"

"Got it, thanks." I said, almost saluting.

"It should be warming up tomorrow, have a great trip."

I had no reason to wait but I did. I instinctively waited to wave goodbye.

I watched the heat from the car's open window create its own fog. Everything you did out here seemed to make more fog.

The window went up and he drove away. His girlfriend in the blue pick-up followed. She gave me a look. It was a look of motherly compassion and concern, probably pity. She waved goodbye without even opening her window and then they were gone. I watched the red halo glow from the taillights and then they were really gone.

I got unbelievably exited. Finally! Now I could channel some of this penned-up energy! I was giddy, I felt like a small child running out to the playground at recess.

Packing took another thirty minutes. My coffee had long gone cold. But my kayak was now loaded, topped off with two dry bags strapped to the stern that didn't fit in the hold. I took the sturdy bow rope and pulled. Nothing happened. I pulled harder and nearly fell backward.

This was a mistake I would have normally caught. The kayak, fully loaded must have weighed well over a hundred pounds. But I wasn't going to unpack it. Not now. It was going in the water as is and it was going in now! The time for patience and prudence was over. With serious effort I gave the rope a *heave-ho!* and managed to move a few inches.

I leaned forward and pulled again. The hull scraped hard on the gravel, I could feel the plastic hull of the kayak forming around the rocks and pebbles like a flat tire.

I was up to my knees in water before the boat floated. In the purple pre-dawn light I checked the launch area for anything I may have dropped. Where I dragged the kayak I saw a line of curled bits of lime green plastic from the kayak's hull. I could have not cared less. I took hold of my paddles, sat down, placed the laminated map for the first day between my legs and with Copeland's *"Fanfare for a Common Man"* playing in my head and a rush of joy filling my chest I was off! Adventure!

A dark, thick wave came over the front of the boat and flooded my seat.

"What the fuck?" I paddled a few more strokes. The boat went down again, it was acting like a submarine. If anyone looked from shore (which now vanished in the fog) I would have looked like a man standing waist deep in the bay holding paddles. This never once occurred to me in all my preparations. But now it seemed that the kayak was so densely packed with gear that it left very little space for air. It was likely as dense as the water it was meant to float on. But that didn't matter to me! Too much had gone into preparation to stop now. I kept on paddling even as the boat dropped inches underwater. My adrenaline would not let me stop. I paddled my submarine out into Chokoloskee Bay!

Then, just as illogically, I stopped and looked back. There was nothing but fog all around me. The launch, the mangroves any shoreline at all had vanished. I stared at my compass and my paddles. My fingers were freezing up my whole body shivered. In spite of all the clothing and wet weather gear I comically sported I was getting colder. As the boat came to a stop in the bay, the bow righted. I leaned back slightly and the bow came up. I paddled a few strokes, like I was in a recliner chair and found the boat performed slightly better though every now and then the bow would take a frightening dip and dig deep enough to make my heart stop.

I wondered if, when I dragged the boat across the gravel, I had scraped a fatal gash into the bottom that now was slowly flooding the hull. If so there was the real chance of sinking and having to swim back to a shore I could not see in cumbersome clothing. I considered the possibility: A sunken boat I could not resurface, no car to drive, and no money to do anything. What's more if a powerboat was in the water now, I was invisible. I was a marine hazard. Worries bloomed in my mind. I let out a tiny laugh. I had only been in the water for five minutes. That tightening rope of anxiety I had preparing for the trip was right.

Then three or four feet above me, the fog magically glowed a bright orange-yellow. The sun had risen and it was lighting up the fog. It was magnificent! I became euphoric! I was suddenly invincible! Who cares if I sank and had to swim to shore in humiliation? I was surrounded by foggy orange sunlight in the middle of Chokoloskee Bay! What better place on Earth was there to be?

I leaned back taking in the resplendent orange sherbet and paddled on renewed.

The exercise warmed my fingers and I became more confident that the boat was performing well. I decided to fold up my anxiety and save it for later.

According to my map, I was looking for a river at the south end of the bay and even in fog I could tell by the calming surface of the water that the bay was narrowing.

Ahead was a glowing light that was not the sunrise. It was the first channel marker standing above the fog as out of place as a science fiction prop. It announced the entrance of the Lopez River and the marker had a number. I looked for it on the map and when I found I there my confidence grew enormously. I knew what I was doing, the boat was still floating and the chance of colliding with a powerboat here was next to impossible. Plus, I was warming up! I guessed the air was now in the tolerable low fifty's, delightful.

The map instructed to angle slightly SSW to find the mouth of the river. I reveled in the game of hitting the bull's-eye. The sun diligently evaporated the fog and I started to see the blue outline of trees ahead. The mouth of the river was plain as the nose on my face. I had been paddling for one hour and ten minutes and I found my first landmark. From here on, I said goodbye to civilization. In my mind I saw the town of Chokoloskee vanish behind a veil of mangroves as I entered the river, a mild current pulling me in.

The Lopez Place was the first campsite on the map, the fog was gone now and the morning warmed up to a crisp mid 60's. I stopped for lunch because there was a place to stop, like I found a historic marker or a scenic overlook.

The homestead was no more than six inches above the water: high ground for this country, a luxury in short supply I would discover in the days ahead. The high ground was not natural. The Calusa tribe was responsible for them, piling enough shells into shallow water to make a mound. Nearly all the homesteads in the Ten Thousand Islands were on old Native American shell mounds.

It became the homestead of Gregorio Lopez in the 20th century. Coincidentally Gregorio and I shared the same birthday, a fact I discovered inscribed on the only structure left, a cistern, where the family scratched a note "child Lopes born April 20, 1892."

I ate my crackers and sardines, peanut butter and carrots spiced with a sweet apple washing it down with my ever-present hot tea.

My eyes wandered the landscape, it was warm and inviting and I had already shed most of the soggy layers of winter clothing. They lay on the kayak drying in the sun. All the preparation had paid off and now it was real. I started to enjoy the sensation of "just being". I looked around the sunny morning island, the sun dappled leaves, the butterflies chasing each other, a single bee's buzzzzzz...The tightening band of tension I had felt over a week of preparations was rapidly releasing its grip.

My first night's camp was "Watson's Place" and I wanted to get there early to check the hull for cuts. I

25

only had a rough idea how long it would take to paddle in such a this-way-then-that-way world.

Before I started I took a moment to shift the heavier gear to the back of the kayak it brought the bow up and then the boat performed 100% better. The river was easy; no confusing side channels or splits and well formed soil banks.

I passed a fisherman piloting a small flats boat, he grinned at me, "You're gonna like what's around the bend..." he said.

It was an alligator napping on a spoil of shells, she must have been at least 18 feet long if not more, longer than the kayak. From my seat in the boat we were almost face-to-face. I passed by quietly. Her head was enormous, but she didn't move.

Around a bend the channel opened and became a wide river and not so far away I saw the unmistakable brown line of a wooden dock reaching out. It was "The Watson Place". I had already arrived at my first camp and it was barely half past noon. It was sunny, I was warm and all the foggy predawn panic seemed light years away.

*

The Watson Place was a fairly large forested island of real soil a foot or more above the river. It felt good to stand on solid ground. I learned later it was haunted ground.

Its history is one of the most bizarre in the Everglades.

Edgar Watson was a solitary figure that arrived in the lawless 1890's Everglades with no family and no history. He kept to himself and was rarely seen and then only on trips to Fort Myers or Chokoloskee for provisions. Rumors sprouted that he was a wanted man, maybe a killer on the run. In the folklore of the day it was rumored that Mr. Watson killed Belle Starr, the famous sharpshooting entertainer.

At the time the Everglades was a sanctuary for fugitives, murderers, Civil War deserters and runaway slaves, anyone who may be of interest to bounty hunters. A person like Edgar Watson would not have raised many eyebrows.

What did raise suspicion was the day a fisherman and his son paddling in the Chatham River found a woman's body floating in the black water. She was carved and gutted. They brought the body to the sheriff who dismissed it saying "That ain't nothin', that place up there is crawling with bodies. There's dead people buried everywhere in them woods of Mr. Watson's."

But the boy had worked for Mr. Watson and he admitted witnessing Mr. Watson killing several workers and burying the bodies on his farm or dumping them in the river. Disemboweling the victims so they would sink.

The sheriff assembled a posse and made a call to the Watson Place. It didn't take long to unearth human remains: arms, legs, skulls and whole skeletons. Everywhere they dug they found graves.

The rough body count came to about a dozen.

It was what folks in Chokoloskee had suspected all along. Mr. Watson was killing his workers rather than paying them. In some cases he even killed the families that came looking for their sons.

When Watson returned from a fishing trip he was surprised a posse of men from town. He said someone else must have killed the woman and as for the bodies, they were just part of the island. There was a scuffle, he pulled his rifle and shot the sheriff dead. The posse returned fire and Mr. Watson was killed.

They dragged Edgar Watson's body downriver to a shell mound and buried it. Later citizens of Chokoloskee dug him up and re-buried him on the mainland, concerned that his decomposed body would come out of his shallow grave and float about on the Chatham River at the whim of the tide.

As an epilogue, a woman who bought the place years later went crazy and tried to burn the house down. She said it was haunted, she said it was full of ghosts.

*

I unloaded the kayak from the dock, set up my tent and built a fire. The fire was purely ornamental which unattended went out on its own. I made lunch of canned meat and noodles. I set the camp stove on the picnic bench and watched the stew heat as if I was a boy with a chemistry set.

Afterwards I cleaned my bowl in the hyper mindful manner of the Zen student and set it aside in the sun to dry.

I pulled the kayak up on the dock and turned it over. I ran my hand along the hull feeling a lot of small scrapes but on the very bottom a rock had carved a gouge about two feet long and an 1/8" deep. Had I seen that at the launch I might have scrubbed the trip. But the piece still hung there: a bright green fiddlehead fern. I got my lighter from the Pelican dry box and slowly melted it back into place. I added a few layers of gray gaffer's tape and welded it tight with the lighter. It looked like hell so I turned it over (mildly embarrassed about the DIY job) and then forgot about it.

Wandering the tiny half an acre of soil that comprised the homestead I found it mostly covered in impenetrable mangrove and invasive Brazilian Pepper, there were no trails, only the patch of clearing I was on, the dock and a cistern. Watson's two-story house had been burned to the ground when the Everglades became a park in 1947. I casually kicked the dirt looking for souvenir nails.

At sunset, the dorsal fins of dolphins cut the serene water of the Chatham River. They would be my constant companions.

A self-portrait of my first night in camp was in order. I laid the camera down squarely on the picnic bench, set the timer and pressed the shutter then ran to the dock paddles in hand. I adopted the classic pose of a civil war era tintype. The chirp the camera made counting the seconds radiated outward with a velvety pulse. It seemed to be the lone sound in the wilderness.

That night the anxiety about the trip drifted off like a morning fog and I slept in a way I would envy in more difficult times to come.

As I woke the serenity was palpable. Nothing seemed to move. The sun came up in a cloudless and dry sky: Band-less purple to pink to orange and when the sun actually appeared, the sky blossomed a yellow-orange and the Everglades warmed and became active.

I packed my gear slowly. Today was a short day, one of the shortest distances of the trip. The itinerary was simple: stick to the west bank of the Chatham River, follow a winding creek to the mouth of Chevalier Bay where, down a channel along the mangrove called Opossum Key or Possum Key, I would find "Darwin's Place" the campsite of day two.

*

The guidebook mentioned that Darwin's Place was built on a Calusa shell mound. Arthur Darwin remained on the property until his death in 1971 when it became part of Everglades National Park. The book said it was possible to find the foundations of the house, but I didn't find any.

I pulled into an indentation in the muddy bank made I'm sure by numerous canoe and kayak landings. Darwin's place looked dour and overused. Tiny multicolored bits of trash were mixed in with trampled brown leaves. It looked like the kind of campsite that rats and raccoons frequented and chewed holes in your precious nylon stuff sacs looking for peanut butter and trail mix. If I thought there was a chance of success, I would have paddled on to another site.

*

Entry from the sketchbook. I am attending a 10-day Zen meditation retreat days before the trip:

"I choose to meditate all night on the final day to see if it is effective. I set up in the guest bedroom breezeway (an area closest to the back door and next to a bathroom. I ended up here because at the last minute my plan created some stir as to where the other people would sleep as several used meditation room to sleep in).

The first three hours (9 to 12) go by quickly, my friend Franklin sitting with me, he left at midnight. Alone at 2:30-3 AM, things got weird. I had an excessive buzzing in my ear, a loud buzzing.

The closet doors to my immediate left dissolved and became a rushing electric waterfall. Within the buzzing sound I heard an operatic voice, wailing a dirge. Out of the waterfall emerged a face- it sang the dirge but where its mouth should have been was only a flat patch of skin."

At this time, I was living in my studios, but the studios were nearly unlivable. Around 10 PM and sometimes as early as 7, the thumping began from the nightclub directly below. The club opened while I was traveling through Southeast Asia. It was fortuitous that Pierre who rented two units in the Art Center had moved to France and left me with all three studios but the noise was disabling and it was driving me crazy. I made plans whenever I could to get out of town just to get eight hours of sleep. It was like having perpetual jetlag. I had to use two types of earplugs at the same time; the foam type topped off with putty-like silicone ones. In combination with over-the-counter sleeping pills desiccating side effects, I managed to plug my ear canal with a solid lump of earwax that left me deaf for three days. It was not healthy.

*

There was a chill in the air before the dawn though thankfully not as cold as the morning on Chokoloskee Bay. I stood on the edge of the dent in the mud where my kayak floated nearly motionless and listened to dolphins in the channel blowing air just beyond my view. The sky was orange-white over the treetops. I made tea and oatmeal and ate it with a cool, sweet apple. I stared at the remnants of candle wax stuck to the wooden picnic table. I packed up my gear giving myself the morning briefing: for the next few days I would be paddling through a series of lakes linked by small channels without much in the way of soil. Channel markers helped confirm where I was but they were not always numbered correctly and I took their appearance with a grain of salt. Once I understood how to interpret the map alone, I did better.

I crossed small Cannon Bay and passed through a channel to oblong Tarpon Bay (to add to a traveler's confusion, there are several *Tarpon Bays* in the Ten Thousand Islands).

On the south end I entered thin Alligator Creek where I saw no alligators though I paddled it for the better part of an hour. I wish I could have paddled it for the rest of my life. It was about the width of a boat slip and my kayak seemed to love its twists and turns. The sun had warmed the air and added a pleasant breeze. Dragonflies hovered over the creek and bees and butterflies fluttered about on wildflowers. My mind drifted into a kind of a trance where everything became crystal clear and beautiful. In the bright noonday sun, diamonds dripped from the tips of my paddles. High in the sky above, pelicans fell into formation and beyond them frigate birds floated lazily this way and that. It was an Eden.

After a cluster of switchbacks, the creek opened up to Alligator Bay and I got my first gusts of steady wind. I kept to the east bank of a peninsula and at the point, the map said I was now in a small bay called "Dad's". I could easily have looped it for the exercise. On the northeast side was the mouth of Gator Bay Canal, a man-made cut that was straight as an arrow. Just ahead, a mangrove island that topped the mouth of Plate Creek like the cork of a wine bottle. Gregorio Lopez named it Plate Creek after losing a plate in the water, plain and simple. I slipped into it joyfully. The little creeks were my favorite.

The map said that the creek had one turn where I would find a creek entering from the left. I made a mental note to confirm it. These confluences were not always so clear. The safest way to stay in the correct creek was to hug the bank opposite the merge. If the other creek came in from the left, I stayed close to the mangroves on the right bank.

The creek evenly widened into a cone-shape. Staying to the right I passed around the island that always corked a channel. Here, the right bank was a peninsula. I turned to point the boat to the south to spot two islands on the far side of Plate Creek Bay. The eastern island would have my chickee. I bee-lined across open water and on the south end, I could already see Plate Creek Bay chickee right where I expected it to be.

A chickee is a platform built above the water where there is no land available to camp on. Originally these would be made of branches, logs, palm thatch and anything that worked. The Calusa, Miccosukee and Tequesta all built chickees. Today the modern forest service chickee is a 10x10' recycled plastic planked platform with a pitched roof and a port-a-potty fastened to a deck about twenty feet away. They are spaced a day's paddle from each other throughout the western Everglades.

Finding the chickee at the end of the day was exquisite. It meant my paddling was over but it also meant my view of the world was accurate.

Several tools combined to make this happen: first, the printed map which was my primary guide. Second the map I kept in my head: the picture of my experience, what the mangroves, creeks and bays looked like in comparison to the map. Third was the time map: where I think I should be according to the where I found these landmarks and where sun was in the sky, even what the animals were doing. Finally there was the map of what I expected to see. When all these matched up and I found the creek, pond or chickee where I expected to find it, it was deeply satisfying. When it didn't, that was a whole other story. There is no trail in the swamp, and so there was always the chance of taking a wrong turn that sends you down a *rabbit hole.*

I've never been in an actual rabbit hole. What I called a rabbit hole in the labyrinth was a wrong turn you take and continued on as if getting to the end of it might offer an answer, even though you know you're lost. The fatal problem is with a rabbit hole is the sense of second-guessing and doubt they nurture. Doubt weakens good decisions and the more time in a rabbit hole the more difficult it becomes to return to the route.

Odds are a novice kayaker in a rabbit hole would find it far too tempting to simply cross a bay or cut through a mangrove imagining that this would get them back on the route. It might work but odds are that it won't. Through experience I learned the only way out of a rabbit hole was to stop, backtrack your route until the landmarks and the map match again, even if it meant going all the way back to "start" -to the chickee, to getting in the kayak first thing in the morning. It was painstaking and time-consuming.

I learned not to get into a rabbit hole in the first place. Being lost causes panic in seconds and panic puts everything into doubt. Retracing your route was the best antidote and solution. Because I had practiced travel through this environment, I never succumbed to the temptation of the rabbit hole, I didn't get lost once in the thirteen days.

As I unloaded the kayak onto Plate Creek chickee, I felt a mild sense of unease. The satisfaction I felt from finding this camp had dissipated and left me wondering if I was paddling through my life doubtful and undirected. The unease I felt returning from Bali, leaving Bali, not entirely certain where the next turn was, was clearly present but I didn't know what to do about it. I had the distinct sensation I may have taken a turn down a rabbit hole. It was a sensation made even worse because I knew myself well enough to know that when opportunities appeared, I often passed them by because I resisted change. I was like a giant ship, once I got going, it was hard for me to turn, even if a far better opportunity appeared. I realized that in my own mind I had rabbit holes too. And I had a history of getting lost and not finding a way out for years. I worried that getting lost in the rabbit hole had become a habit.

I made a simple note of this feeling in my sketchbook. I promised myself to dig onto the self-analysis later, but I never did.

*

The next day I would be paddling through Lostman's Bay and I took heed of the name.

"Lostman's Bay: Is it metaphor for life?" I wondered out loud like a BBC presenter.

I considered the thought. Whereas a poor choice in life might result in doldrums of obscurity and insignificance, loosing ones way in the swamp likely put a quick end to your story. I decided the metaphor didn't hold up.

The wilderness did not take pity on mistakes. It just killed. There are plenty of stories of Everglades fishermen finding a boat containing a desiccated and half eaten body of lostmen, sometimes found less than a mile from safety. If the dead could have bee-lined over the maze of mangroves they would have easily survived. But confusion can be as deadly as anything else. And the labyrinth had that in spades.

Hell's Bay, Lostman's Bay, Lostman's Key, Big Lostman's Bay, Lostman's Five Bay, they weren't just names, they were stories.

"Five English sailors had deserted their post in Key West and paid a local fisherman to help them escape. He left them on an island at the mouth of a river telling them they would find a town on the eastern end. The sailors never found the town. The fisherman had cruelly tricked them out of their money. There was no town on Lostman's Key. A few weeks later, William Allen found them nearly starved to death and took them to Punta Gorda."

*

That night I no dreams came to call and that was a relief. Because if the sandman had sprinkled his dust, I would have surely have had nightmares.

In the morning my packing was easy and efficient. I was already lighter by two gallons of drinking water and a pound or two of food. Now there was a cubic foot of free space in the hold, a cavern. I started to think ahead and layer the gear for what would come next: food bags on top, fresh water always handy, clothes bag followed by the tent, the camp stove. My meditation gear was packed with my clothes except for the bell I rang to begin and conclude meditations, it was in the Pelican box where I could deploy it to ring when I found myself in particularly spiritual surroundings. Beyond that was gear stowed for the coming days. Finally I balanced the load so perfectly as to make the kayak float a little higher at the bow. Loading became an art.

*

The morning was rapidly warming up. I donned a t-shirt and shorts that now nearly hung off me. I had paddled my way down to my high school body. I slid the boat off the deck. It spooned into the calm water sending a round wave far out into Plate Creek Bay. I took a last look-around for anything I might have forgotten. I found a candleholder, a bungee cord and a bit of plastic trash.

Plate Creek Bay was momentarily windless. I sat in the kayak rubbing the stalk of my wood paddles with just the right amount of water. Not more than two hundred yards away and in plain view was the channel I would start with. Today would be one of the longest days yet. Even though it measured only six-miles on the map, there was no straight line to it. It was nearly all time swallowing, confounding labyrinths. And there was no way of measuring how long it would take to make it to camp.

Halfway across the Bay, I spotted the straight, white lines of a dock: it was the Lostman's Five campsite and I pulled in to make a hot breakfast. Any solid ground was worth a stop but campsites were never as clean as a chickee. Ground camps always had a clutter of tiny plastic bits in the leaves and dirt. Most common were the pieces of candy wrappers followed by the plastic rings from bottle tops and bottle caps. All the things people found too small and tedious to pick up. Lostman's Five had the look of regular visitors: raccoons, squirrels and possibly rats. I wondered if, like me, other paddlers chose the cleaner, breezier and bug-free chickee.

I tied off to the mangroves, there was no sign anyone had been here recently. I wondered how long it had been vacant, the shallow water just before this site would cut out most of the fishing boat traffic, and few people decided or had the chance to take a thirteen-day kayak trip. I guessed that no sign of recent visitors meant I was not following anyone. In a way, I had the Everglades to myself.

I moved on quickly after breakfast paddling to the channel and entering Two Island Bay. On the west bank the map showed a creek. Expecting it to be a refuge from the wind that would pick up later, I took it.

Mid-way down the creek, I passed through a beautiful and shallow pond. When I got to the other side I turned to look back. My trail told a story, a line of brown with flowerlike blossoms on either side where my paddles dug.

It struck me that a shallow, muddy pond could be dangerous if one ran aground. I began to think of the possibilities. This kind of mud surface is an illusion. It's more like a thin brew of silt that is denser the deeper down you get until it is as thick as a mud puddle on a rainy forest trail. Try to stand on it and you would sink. The mud would form tightly around your legs. Mud like that sticks and it wouldn't let you out. The more you struggle, the tighter the grip. I continued my thought experiment. I imagined one chance of escape would be to float to shore doing a breaststroke and dragging a line to a solid bank and pulling the kayak out to some deeper water. Though as I thought about it, likely a leg would dip into the mud and get caught. No, I don't think that would work. Better to be on your guard when around mud and avoid it altogether. The ranger at the park headquarters warned about mud.

The creek drained into a channel. Immediately ahead was a mangrove island and another larger island behind it. Now I understood some of the natural construction of the labyrinths. As a channel poured into a bay, it deposited mud and sand where eventually a patch of land formed, after so many years, mangroves colonized it and made an island. So each and every channel and creek with enough flow would produce a minor delta. The process went on over and over, delta after delta until ten thousand little islands were formed.

When I was very young, I used to spend my days along the creeks in the forest behind my home. I would build dams, fish traps and dig channels. I built miniature homes with sticks and leaves. I dug holes and made muddy ponds and to tried to stock them with fish. Every now and then I would turn over a flat rock and expose a beautiful red ochre crawfish. We called them crawdads, there is no etymology on the name but just the sound of it can spirit me back to that time playing in the creeks in dreamlike detail.

Almost as soon as my family moved to the rural Ohio countryside where I played in hundreds of acres forest, the bulldozers arrived to scrape it off and build a sprawling subdivision of homes. I often wonder if that had never happened, would I be spending my life looking for a home, the kind of home that doesn't change? That isn't plowed over or invaded? My parents were probably thinking the same thing when they bought the house. They had both experienced their entire young life being plowed over by Blitzkrieg. They lived under Nazi occupation in Poland for six years, my mother only two miles away from Auschwitz.

"They're burning bodies over there," she told her younger sister looking out the window at the distant smokestacks.

My mother was no longer talking about the war. She had just started on an intramuscular dose of Haldol, a powerful anti-psychotic that was effective for six months and it performed a miracle.

For years my family had been suffering along with my mother and the mental illness that destroyed her. In the mid 1980's when I was living in Boston my father called me from Michigan to tell me that he found my mother and was leaving for England to bring her home. I didn't know she was missing. My father didn't tell anyone. Not the police, not my brother who lived in Detroit, and as far as I knew, he told no one at work.

He didn't know what had happened to her either, just that the car was missing. It wasn't until a friend he had not heard from for thirty years called to say that she was in a hotel room in London unhappy and crying and very disturbed.

My mother had slowly been going insane. Voices were taunting her about the safety of the children. Super-secret organizations had built underground listening facilities below the house. And one day she learned that this secret organization planned to blow the house up while she was inside.

She bought a one-way ticket to London flying out of Toledo, she left a message on my brother Chris' answering machine to come and take care of the dog (though no message was recorded) and drove away.

Sometimes I would answer the phone and I would hear my mother already mumbling to someone. To her the phone was always active, someone was already listening whether you dialed a number or not. My heart sank when I got those calls because I knew I would be flying home to do something unspeakable, commit my mother to a mental institution.

My father brought her back for what turned out to be nearly fifteen years of hell. Years later he told me, in passing, that she had been cutting and pasting together messages from magazines like ransom notes.

They were frightening notes about people wanting to do harm to her or us.

"Is this really you, Mark?" she would ask when I called, checking if I had been replaced by an imposter.

Time and time again, when it was my turn, I had to fly in to see a judge and commit my mother to a mental ward. We took turns my father, brother and I. My mother never took the medications she was given by court order, so in about two months she would have another breakdown.

She would have horrifying episodes. Vindictive voices tormented her and told her to kill herself, and once she took the advice. But my father happened to come home early, found her and pulled her head out of the oven where the gas had put her to sleep.

Dr. Marcotti one of her psychiatrists, said once that the source of everything she was dealing with came from the War, the Nazi occupation, the poison and fear imprinted on an adolescent mind: paranoid-schizophrenia as a symptom of post-traumatic-stress-disorder.

Her escape just after Germany surrendered when Poland was swallowed into the Russian Zone is light on details. I was too young to ask my grandfather before the Alzheimer's took his memory and my mother's stories about the period were mixed with other stories from my childhood. My aunt was too young when it happened to understand what was going on. Still, piece-by-piece a picture appears.

Just before the invasion of Poland in September 1939, my grandfather, a conscripted soldier, left the family to fight in the useless defense of Poland. He vanished for the duration of the war. In fact he was taken prisoner by Stalin's army where he sat out the conflict for two years until he was put him into service in a multi national force confronting Rommel in Persia and North Africa.

Somewhere in the Kurdish mountains the corps found an orphaned bear cub and adopted him as a pet. (That was the story told to me but other sources say they bought the bear at a railroad station on Hamadan, Iran.)

Today I wear a ring that my grandfather bought during the war. We know this because in his things my aunt also found a silver cigarette case with a mosque drawn into it. Words scratched into the soft silver read "Teheran".

We have black and white photos of my grandfather standing in the dinner line jokingly wrestling with the bear (his name was Wojtek).

When the Polish II Corps saw battle in Monte Cassino, Italy, the bear helped carry the heavy artillery. Being brought up in the military he thought he was a soldier like everyone else.

From Italy my grandfather hired the underground to smuggle his family out of Poland.

In the meantime, my grandmother did what she could. She found a job in a bakery for the years of occupation hoping that at least she could be near food.

One day after the war ended, and she had long given up on her husband, someone came to her house and told her there was a package at the post office for her. It had been there for quite some time.

When she got it home, she opened it and found a moldy fruitcake inside. But there was no wasting it, that evening she cut slices for tea and found a note inside. It said a person would come to the house and that she should do what this person says. She recognized the handwriting. Against all odds her husband had survived the war and was now going to get them out.

Moments later there was a knock at the door.

A man entered acting like an old friend, sat and asked for tea. While they ate the fruitcake he laid out a plan: she would go alone to the train station. The children would walk together down the street to play in the schoolyard, and they should act like children: singing and holding hands. Leave everything in the house, carry nothing, leave the lights on and tell no one, they should begin in ten minutes. Then he left.

My grandmother followed instructions immediately. When she got to the train station, another man passed by and whispered, *"Come with me"*. She followed him to a car. The children were already inside. They drove away. The man gave them documents, papers and passports, they were to be the "Gold" family and they had been in hiding throughout the war and were now traveling to Palestine, to join their family living in Jerusalem.

At the border of Czechoslovakia, they met another *"Come with me"* person, this time a woman. She gave instructions: my young aunt would go with a lady across the border bridge, they would tell the border guard that they were mother and child going to attend temple on the other side. Meantime my mother and my grandmother would walk through the forest and ford the river at a shallow spot they would have to find themselves.

My aunt crossed into Czechoslovakia without a hitch and was brought to a waiting room in family home. Meantime my grandmother and mother stared at a river swollen with rainfall and high wherever they looked. My grandmother argued with my mother about crossing. She was afraid of drowning in the swirling brown water. Their loud talking attracted the attention of a passing border guard and they were taken to jail.

My aunt was left weeping in the room alone. No one in the family came to console her. That was the way of the underground: if you didn't see a face you couldn't identify them. She didn't know what had happened to her family, she was only nine years old.

As the shifts changed, a superior officer arrived at the jail looked at my grandmother's (counterfeit) papers, believed them to be authentic and had the boarder guard escort them to the border bridge. In the street on the other side they noticed the woman who gave them instructions and followed behind her until they reached the house where my aunt was being kept.

When my grandmother and her daughters crossed into Italy my grandfather was there to greet them. I have in my collection the picture of that moment. They are standing in front of a huge military transport truck, my grandfather wearing the Polish II Corps uniform, a cigar between his fingers. Grandmother stands in front, her head tilted towards his smiling. My sixteen-year-old mother in a skirt and white blouse and my aunt looking much younger than her nine years in a short white dress. They are clustered together like they would never allow anyone to wedge them apart ever again.

*

I waited until the compass needle settled directly south then pointed the bow across Onion Key Bay to an island. When I reached it, I slipped into a wide channel that snaked through the mangroves, chagrined that it didn't stop the wind.

I came out on Third Bay, pulled up snug against the mangroves to study the map. Just then the wind whipped and nearly snatched it out of my wet hand. I felt the instant flood of panic in my chest. I imagined watching the map skitter across the surface of the bay and slowly sink like a leaf into the deep, brown water.

To loose the map would have been catastrophic. I would be left to navigate with the simple map included in the package the ranger handed me along with my itinerary and rules of power boating in manatee zones. I decided to tie my maps to a line but I never did.

I was getting hungry (I was always hungry!) but I couldn't find a patch of ground anywhere to stop and eating on the water was out of the question. The food was stowed. I needed at least one square foot of solid bank where I could stand up an open the hatch without a threat of a wave pouring in.

The map showed a swirl of creeks ahead that passed in and out of the mangroves. I might find a beach there.

I headed down the very first creek and found a miniscule patch of soil no bigger than home plate. I pulled up, hooked the bow in the mangrove branches and hopped out. Standing and stretching my legs felt exquisite (It felt good to get out of the kayak, it felt good to get in).

I opened a tin of sardines, and laid out a buffet of crackers, peanut butter and applesauce on the stern of the boat. I looked at my feet now sinking into the tiny mound of soil, a footprint for the ages, maybe. Maybe mine would be the footprints an archaeological student would find 30,000 years from now. The sea would certainly reclaim this area by then, it was rapidly on its way. The Everglades was a landscape that appeared and vanished under the waves many times in expanse of geologic time.

I carefully undid the bungee cords holding the watertight Pelican box strapped to the top of the bulkhead and took out my camera. I would have liked getting to the camera to be easier. I scolded myself for not buying a few disposable waterproof cameras. They would have been perfect. A cheap camera in the hand beats a good one stowed away any day.

As I took the selfie, the place revealed itself. When the shutter clicked, my mind spread wide. I stood in a maze of creeks, ponds and bays far enough from any town to be out of cell phone reception and impossible to walk out of. Being lost here meant a slow death. Losing the boat was sure death. No fishing boat would pass by and find me here. I did the thought experiment: the soonest I could expect help was via search helicopter and a search would not begin for at least eight days. Not until the harbormaster at Flamingo Marina noticed the keys dated February 6 still hanging on a hook.

And yet, I felt giddy with the sensation of solitude and freedom. Not the reaction one might expect weighing the chances of survival and coming up short.

*

The creek returned to Third Bay. I kept to the southeast bank passing through a wide channel and navigating around a cluster of islands skirting Big Lostmans's Bay.

On the map I took notice of a long thin line that spurred of near where I was. It was a creek hardly noticeable from the bay, just a sideways gap in the mangroves four feet wide. As I entered, the wind vanished and I was greeted by the scent of blooming flowers and dancing butterflies. On a muddy bank, an unconcerned flock of white egrets waded. The mangroves were short and the sunlight streaked the submarine world with lines of yellow and green. I could see the roots of lily pads and white shells on the creek bed. The kayak drifted along in a light current without the need of the paddles.

When I came out, I was in Lostman's Five Bay and faced the largest piece of open water since Chokoloskee four days ago. I shoved the map deeper under my seat and headed east-southeast across open water looking for the island (the cork island?) that would identify the entrance to my next creek.

By now it was mid-afternoon, my meanderings through creek after creek had eaten up valuable time and left little to find tonight's chickee. I felt a mild sense of anxiety. A state of mind that I would later learn could be fatal. Anxiety, doubt, panic, all were conditions I would later study when I learned how dangerous they could be.

The creek appeared almost mystically and I paddled through it quickly to a breezy Roger's River Bay. I expected the chickee to be on the left but it wasn't there. The sun was low in the west. I didn't need this right now. Had I made a mistake? Where was the error? How far back? Which bay was this? It wasn't large, maybe it wasn't on the map, or wasn't a bay at all but just a widening of the creek. Where was I?

I paddled along the northwest shore keeping an eye for any straight lines, the unnatural tattoo of human construction: beams, decks and the artificially green color of the port-a-potty.

Perhaps if the day was young I might have been amused, but now the sun was setting and once it did, darkness came on rapidly. Complete darkness.

Without light I could easily pass by a chickee that would be in plain view in daylight. The beam of a headlamp only went so far and it made everything flat, which was its own disorienting distortion. It would be impossible to find a chickee in the dark. I estimated less than an hour of light, probably closer to half an hour.

Hugging the shoreline wasn't working so I paddled out into the bay. I glanced behind me and saw something unusual. I let the kayak come about. There it was: The chickee nestled in the wide concave bight of Roger's River Bay. I studied the map. It was not where the mapmaker put it. The mapmaker placed the chickee in the tiny bight closest to the mouth of the creek. In fact it was a good 100 yards away hidden from view by a thin peninsula of mangroves. It was a minor error but one that could be dangerous depending on a kayaker's state of mind at the time, and I was close to that state. With emphasis I circled this error in red marker meaning to call the cartographer when I returned to the world.

I let out a great sigh of relief: Dinner and sleep was in sight. Later, in my tent, I read about this site in the guidebook. *"...entering Roger's River Bay from the north, the chickee is hidden by mangroves, paddle out and turn around in order to find it".* I changed my mind about guidebooks.

That night I tossed and turned not finding a comfortable spot on the wood deck, I considered getting up and rigging my hammock to sleep in then, somehow, I fell into a deep sleep.

In my dream, I stood on a riverbank in a forest, my kayak nearby. I noticed dark clouds and went to pitch my tent but could only find a flat blue sheet. Downriver a few people arrived on a big barge that broke the solitude. I saw just to the left of my camp the riverbank had fallen flat and it seemed that many people had walked there and flattened a wide path. A man in his thirties came by in a golf cart. As we talked RVs appeared across the river. He said there was going to be a big outdoor festival. I asked how far I would have to go to find a wild place on the river. While we talked, the river dried up and became a dusty roadway. Large brick houses were being built on the other bank and huge trucks jammed the dry, dusty riverbed roadway.

*

In the pale canopy of light just before dawn, I crouched over the map. The dream had left me feeling an anger and anxiety that I could do nothing with. I've had that dream many times. Each time I am in the forest or a yard or a park when huge trucks arrive and start tearing up the landscape pushing the good things in the world aside. I am left with a sour sense of having lost something beautiful that will never return.

I follow the day's route with the tip of a pencil. Today is day five. For the most part, I will be paddling rivers easily navigated, Roger's River Bay chickee to Broad River camp, it was the closest I would get to the waves and tides of the Gulf of Mexico. In fact for the next two and a half days I would travel only on rivers, the maze of mangroves was over for now.

I took a picture of the dawn from Roger's River chickee and later pasted it in my sketchbook. Purple with pink edges, a light fog softening the mangrove peninsula, the water utterly motionless: a reflective sheen like polished glass.

There was really no navigation to do. Ahead only one decision to make; take a large channel to Broad River or a thin, winding creek. I would choose the creek.

I cleared the chickee, filled my mug with Chinese tea and sat down in the kayak. I put my hands in the familiar spot on the paddles. I pointed the bow at the end of the small peninsula that hid the chickee from me last night, and paddled out for Cabbage Island, an island so imposing that it looked like part of the south shore.

Identifying islands or channels from a distance required a combination of subtle awareness, intuition and the outright guess. The view from a kayak in a bay was nothing more than a great deal of brown water and a lot of sky, hopefully blue. Between the two like a folded ripple in the universe was a thin fringe of green spongy foliage. With a good eye and patient Indian staring (looking from the side rather straight on) you could distinguish the misty-white green fringe from the slightly darker green fringe indicating space between the two.

The bay was still windless at this time of the morning and the kayak skimmed across the top of the water effortlessly. I came to the tip of the peninsula then pointed my kayak thirty degrees to the right towards the whiter patch of green. A wide wake spread as I crossed the flat water. I loved the morning. It was a soundless and motionless world as still and silent as a photograph.

I reached Cabbage Island in fifteen minutes and paddled along the west side into the channel between the island and the mangroves. As it widened, I turned east into a cone shape that funneled down to the creek. This was all the navigation I had to do today, I could have stowed the map.

The creek was even more beautiful than the others. It was thin, deep and clear. I paddled through the dwarf mangroves close enough to touch them. I arrived at a confluence, another creek on the west bank, I knew from studying the map that it was short and ended in a tiny pond. I imagined a shallow mud-filled pool, a La Brea tar pit waiting for some daydreaming kayaker to wander into. And like all dead ends, they had their own siren calls. They called for you with their beautiful voice.

I paddled with the mild current: the river of grass flowing to the sea. I felt the thin expanse run off the giant sand belly of Florida. The cast spell of light and silence. A whisper of a breeze tapped the mangroves leaves while dragonflies flew this way and that. Spiders beautiful in their own harmless way floated on their webs. And as my paddles came over my head I watched in wonder the line of drops cascading like diamonds in the sun. The creek may have only been a mile long, but it took me light years away, long and far from thoughts of distance and navigation. I was hypnotized. The gentle curves, shimmering water, the midday silence. I was immersed, paddling in a state of samadhi.

From the sketchbook:

I watched the paddle lift high in brother sky

Where it caught the tiny silk line of a spider

In the time it took for the paddle to pinwheel to the water

Spider cast the line,

Cut it, and sailed off on the winds.

While you were sleeping,

Water squirts from his mouth, he turned,

Rolled on the surface,

And disappeared under the boat.

Leaving a single siren call announcing

A past of dreams.

A present of dreams.

A future of dreams.

While you were sleeping,

The newborn came forth breaking the surface and filling the

Air with a salty aroma.

A caul drifted off in the waves.

On the shore, holding the breath that no one would recover,

A solitary girl stands in the wind of a thousand lifetimes,

Flower petals flutter by her face golden and

Crimson in the retiring sun.

"I will take to the air," she said,

"On wings of hope and longing,

"Come with me and sing of the multitudes,

"Of the 10,000 things."

And she nestled squarely on the cupped hands

Of past and future.

In a bird's nest of sea oats, marl and guano.

The sun set the sky alight,

And diamonds cascaded off your paddle.

A precious constant pedigreed in the universe of

Coming and going, coming and going

Repeating a sound that echoed off the

Distant clouds and into the blossoming sky,

Evermore,

  Evermore,

   Evermore.

*

The creek curled like a fishhook. It was the curve that announced the entrance to Broad River and looming over the mangroves something extraordinary: a large white sail levitating downriver. The image was nearly mystical. I was just paddling out of the creek when I saw the sailboat itself and it was every bit as whimsical in full view as the sail was alone.

It was a long, clearly hand-made thing piloted by a man at the rudder. The boat looked to be thirty-feet stem to stern and shaped like a badly rolled cigarette or some long thin lumpy pastry yet to be put in the oven. I guessed it was made of fiberglass sheets. It more than reminded me of a Dr. Zeuss drawing. *It was a Dr. Zeuss drawing come to life.*

The head of a woman on a pillow, her eyes shut sleeping in the bow, was the only passenger. The man who held the outrageously large rudder pole didn't seem to notice me. They moved along like a hovering apparition and passed by so quickly I didn't have time to wave, say hello or take a photo. In a matter of minutes the fairy vessel was out of sight, sail and all.

I stopped paddling to drift and let the dream continue. At that moment had a glowing mermaid surface and hand me a multi-colored mushroom I would not have been surprised in the least.

I felt the current take me on my long, lazy drift down Broad River towards the Gulf of Mexico. Still craving the intimacy of the small creek, I hugged mangroves along the north shore but it wasn't the same. Moments later I passed by the alternate routes, The Cutoff: a channel that crossed from Roger's River to the Broad.

I faced directly into the afternoon sun and it reflected off the water something fierce. I had a hard time looking in the direction I was going so I kept my eyes off to the side and my hat down. Compared to the docile creek, this was downright awful. As much as I could I kept behind the shade of the mangroves.

It took an hour, but the sun mercifully settled and the left bank became festooned in tall mangroves, buttonwood and cypress trees. Then, a small whitewashed dock and a happy brown sign displaying a white tent symbol, it was the Broad River campsite. A canoe was tethered to the post. I stopped paddling and let my kayak drift. I preferred ending the day's paddle silently. Meanwhile I cleared my throat preparing to use my voice again.

I stepped up on the high, solid ground (a bluff nearly three feet above the water!) I wondered what enterprising Calusa built this shell mound.

The canoe belonged to a young German couple. They were friendly enough but mostly kept to themselves.

The campsite was big enough to allow this without any awkwardness and our communication added up to a few waves and smiles. Perhaps they chose to keep a kind of noble silence. It was not uncommon to find this characteristic in the wild. Awe of the silence where nature is present and palpable, it was the noble silence of respect.

As I set up my tent, I considered the two choices I had tomorrow, but I already knew what I would do.

Choice #1: paddle Broad River out to the coastline then south in the open gulf waters to the mouth of the Harney River where I would re-enter the Everglades. That choice might take me through an interesting and different ecosystem, but it also had its perils. On the coast there was no knowing how strong or the direction of the wind. Nor could you say how rough the water might be. Looking at the satellite view, the shore seemed quite shallow and that meant shallow mud and sand. On the other hand, a wild Florida coastline strewn with swirling sand islands is rare and could be terrifically interesting.

Instead, what beckoned to me from the map was choice #2: *"The Nightmare"*, a wispy thread of connected canals, creeks and ponds traversing the dense mangrove forest. If I navigated it correctly, I would come to the end of a creek and find the Harney River chickee.

The challenges with this route were numerous and listed in the guidebook. In fact, it was the only time I found the guidebook essential because embedded in the description of "The Nightmare", was a tide chart.

The Nightmare could only be traversed during high tide. That explained the depth gage next to the Broad Creek dock. If you calculated right, high tide gave you about four hours to successfully pass through the shallows of "The Nightmare".

The guidebook instructed to allow a delay of 1.5 hours as the tidewater flowed in and out of the spongy mangroves. Then the guidebook gave a last warning:

> *"Miss the timing and you may be caught in water too shallow to paddle until the return of high tide which could be overnight, an impossible time to travel without becoming lost. Therefore you would likely have to wait twelve hours for the next daylight tide. Paddlers should be prepared for the possibility."*

Meaning you might have to spend the night in "The Nightmare" with whatever real or imagined creatures inhabit the swamp.

I familiarized myself with the water gage and tried to calculate the time, but it wasn't so easy. In fact it was bloody confusing. It seemed to cause instant dyslexia, (is the water rising or is it falling? Is my note right or did I write it wrong?) Tides are subtle as they arrive inland and I wasn't confident with my conclusion or the guidebook's.

It was subtle but the river itself gave me a better clue. The current seemed to be moving *in* not *out* to sea. I tossed a few floaters out in the middle and watched them, they moved inland with the current; the tide was coming in. It was a 'bore', the rising tide pushing the river inland (I am taking some license with the meaning, an actual *bore* is a relatively large wave in a river caused by the incoming tide. A good read is Somerset Maugham's short story *"The Bore"* about surfing a bore on the island of Borneo). I made some notes and calculated that the best time to head into The Nightmare was 9:30 tomorrow morning.

With the kayak mostly empty, I decided to have a look-see at "The Nightmare". The entrance was less than a quarter-mile downriver. What I found was a large pond completely still and full of dead, sun-bleached tree trunks standing out of the brown water. This was the entrance to "The Nightmare" and, as I paddled in, alligators and turtles leapt off the bent tree trunks with a startling funhouse splash.

There were many alligators, maybe 100, a lot of alligators. This place was like a child's horror fantasy. A Disney animated version of a nightmare. The water was deep and I was very glad to be in a boat. Deep, opaque water always gave me the chills. Being so close to the salty Florida Bay, I could easily be in crocodile territory and that was a concern. Crocs were far, far more dangerous than gators.

I have been around plenty of alligators and never considered them a threat. They sleep all day, don't eat in the winter and are generally shy of people. But this many big reptiles was making me nervous and if there were any crocodile, well, that was a whole different story and no one would hear your screams out here. Regardless of what reptile we talk about, they're all territorial and if they feel boxed it, good luck.

On the east side of the lagoon I found the entrance to "start here" creek. The winding route through the labyrinth that would eventually bring me to Broad Creek (not Broad River, don't get confused) and the portion presumably shallow enough to dry up at low tide.

Nearby was another tempting creek called Wood Creek. Unlikely as it was, if I mistakenly took that creek, I would be paddling on and on, deeper and deeper into the Everglades until the creek just stopped. There would have been no clue until that sudden end. And that may have been after three hours of unsuspecting paddling.

If I paddled up Wood Creek (and paddled back out), I would have used up my high tide and would have no choice but to return to the Broad River campsite and try "The Nightmare" again the next day. More likely I would have chucked it and taken the coastal route instead.

I told myself to be extra careful not to take Wood Creek tomorrow, even though it was obviously the wrong way.

The abundance of caution was because of a conversation with a geologist who was returning from a week in the Incan silver mines a few years ago.

"Petosi was where most of the Incan silver was extracted and its high altitude mining," he said. "You can find interior cracks in the mountain with vertical drops of a thousand feet or more. Stunning!"

"Alongside the precipice of these drops there's often a shrine to the little troll that lives there. The one that waits for you to look over the edge and teases you saying: 'Jump!' 'No, don't jump!' 'Yes! Jump!'"

Mining accidents were routinely blamed on this cave deity and this was the troll I was concerned about, the one that would, against all logic, confound me into going down Wood Creek.

I paddled back to camp. The sun had already dipped below the trees. I cooked dinner hastily wondering if I had only brought cans of chili on this trip. My neighbors made dinner from bags they kept inside a barrel-size blue plastic drum with a giant screw-on top, clearly an item the outfitters talked them into. Casually, I read the ingredients on the can of chili. It said there was 67% of the daily allowance of salt per serving. There were two serving per can. Ridiculous. I could have easily devoured 2 cans that night providing me with 268% of my daily salt requirement. I could go salt-free for the next 3 days and be fine.

I felt a sting on the tip of my finger, then a nasty itch right in my tear duct.

No-see-ums! The deplorable miniscule biting flies! I felt stinging on my lips, nose and ears, even the rim of the eyelids. Then they were all over me. I watched my German campmates start to swat at the air. Aha! The nightmare had begun! Broad River camp was infested with swarms of biting gnats! They couldn't have picked a worst time: right in the middle of dinner with everything out. I ate as fast as I could, ran to the dock and scooped water into the pot, I'd deal with the clean up later. I leapt into my tent, zipped it up and proceeded to smash and slap the last of the biting flies into oblivion.

I stared at all the no-see-ums trying to get through my tent screen, kudos for good camping gear (expensive but worth it). I fashioned my sleeping bag and ground pad into a Zafu, crossed my legs and sat in meditation until the insidious buzzing dissipated from the tent screen.

The pesky bugs were gone in half an hour. In the wild, bugs have their schedule. Bats and carnivorous insects keep things in check.

I got out and tidied up the campsite. I flashed a light on the tide gauge by the dock. It was of no help. The river seemed to be at the same height as when I arrived. I got back in my tent and pulled out the guidebook flipping to the tide chart, again I made the simple calculation: high tide on January 30, 2000 is expected at 08:37, add the 1.5 hours to reach me, about 10 AM and I can leave early and be travelling through while the tide is filling in the dreaded muddy passages. Embarking at 9:30 sounds perfect.

I lay in bed second-guessing my calculations until I fell asleep.

*

I was up before the sunrise nearly weightless with anticipation. I made breakfast and wandered around without a place to channel my energy. I checked the water gage a hundred times. For some reason just after 7 AM the current noticeably headed upstream. I felt a flush of panic.

It was hours before I expected high tide. What was happening? I stared at the gage with its notches and numbers and imagined the water was already up over one of the more pronounced black notches on the seemingly accurate measuring stick. Of course! The tide is rising! It rises for six hours to high tide...you can leave now. You could have left three hours ago! I broke camp and I did it in short order.

I got in the water so fast it made my neighbors suspicious: should they also be rushing to the river, after all I was the local, maybe I knew something.

"Don't worry, I just have to get through The Nightmare before low tide. Its me, not you," I explained like I was breaking up with them.

"Enjoy your trip!" I said as I paddled off. How strange I thought, to have a conversation with them only when I am leaving. I don't remember them responding to anything I said. It was like saying hello to someone in an elevator who doesn't respond.

The scary pool at the entrance looked completely different. Now in the bright light of morning it was beautiful and inviting. There was none of the foreboding sense of doom from last night. All the alligators were gone, likely snoozing underwater.

I took the cut to the left, leaving Troll's Creek behind (Wood Creek officially but by now I had my own names for everything) I paddled through thinner and thinner ponds connected by deep channels.

Within half an hour I came to my first blocked creek. Dead ahead was a solid wall of mangroves. What have I done?

I idled there looking for a hint of a current. Maybe the creek continued under the web work of mangrove roots, branches and limbs. The bow of the kayak was pulled under some branches, I snapped apart the kayak paddle, tucked them in on either side, leaned back and did a limbo crawl, getting as low as I could and pulling myself along grabbing one branch after another.

I passed through a scrim of webs. Spiders scurried along the roots. I swear I could hear the clack-clack of their spindly legs on the dead wood.

I had to learn to love spiders on this trip, especially the Everglades Spider, a spider as long as the palm of my hand with black with yellow stripes. They poured off the mangroves.

I didn't panic about the spiders. But the branches pushed and yanked at the boat threatening to capsize me, and that did cause alarm. If I fell out, I would not only have to keep hold of the kayak but the current could easily pull me into the twisted mangrove roots that could snag and drown me.

I slipped into an open pond and shook of the bugs. The map showed I would meet up with another creek somewhere soon but there were no landmarks here, nothing to distinguish a creek from a tributary. I had to rely on my inner time-clock and the compass hoping that any of these ponds were part of a delta, part of

The Nightmare and would eventually lead me to Broad Creek.

On the map, one creek stayed in The Nightmare while others went out to the coast. But I wanted to remain in The Nightmare. The map showed a creek appearing after a tight oxbow. I should look for it on my left and follow it.

When I lived on the Big Island we used to joke that driving counterclockwise, everything was on the left. If you drove the coast road you got so tired pulling the wheel to the left all day that you had to turn around and go back the way you came for a while just to unwind.

I found Left Creek immediately after the tight oxbow. But it was tiny. Had I not been keeping an eye out for it, I wouldn't have given this forlorn trickle a second look. It was so shallow I got out of the boat and walked a few paces to see if there was creek here at all. Then I stopped. Standing alone only a few paces from the boat I felt oddly disconnected from my body, I stood in the middle of what seemed to be an endless tangle of mangroves dusted in green mold. I turned to look at the boat, expecting as if in a dream it would not be there. Disappearing into nature, this subtle condition when the forest silence mingled with the playful imagination of the mind. This ineffable condition, I think I was looking it for it all along in my journeys into the wild.

In the stories of the Buddha, he sat under the bodhi tree deciding to not get up until he attained enlightenment. As he struggled with the hindrances of his mind, he remembered a time as a child when he sat in a field just watching the seeds float in the breeze and the clouds pass. He felt no separation between the natural world and himself, he felt the he was *it* and *it* was *he.* And with this memory, the story goes on, he softened his meditation and fell into a deep samadhi.

From the sketchbook of the Pissarro Atelier, France

You asked me to paint you,

But did you know that you would not survive the summer winds?

When all the old man said was that the gate to the deathless was open,

And now looking back,

I remember the one shining moment when we both saw it together,

How we shook with elation at our discovery.

We took to the ether on wings of hope and longing

Singing of the 10,000 things, of the Mahamudra,

Nestled squarely on the cupped hands of past and future,

We found a bird's nest to curl up in

And cuddle in the sea oats, marl and guano.

Finding, but not revealing.

Fearing the whole thing would fold up and blow away if we uttered a word.

We held our breath and kept quiet.

Gazing into the gem, we were blinded,

Or not blinded, but,

Seeing for the first time we broke

Into silence.

Together,

We chose to keep it as it was

As silence

The silence of things being and not being.

The silence of longing and mercy.

Fate and coincidence,

Past and volition,

The good fight and all its painted ministries.

While it was still in sight, I sent an arrow into the center of its space and time.

But once I did,

I could no longer,

feel it

or

find it.

*

I could see sunlight ahead. I pulled the kayak over the shallow, sandy delta to where the creek resumed, took my seat and pulled through another limbo. I popped out into a tiny sun-filled pond that seemed to be the end of the creek. Who divined a trail through this mess? Was The Nightmare just a series of disheartening dead ends that only look like dead ends but were not, each with their own variety of discouraging moments? I wanted to change the name.

Suppressing a cascade of second thoughts, I pushed on through the mangrove tangle into an area of fallen trees in deep water. The white trunks reached out of the lagoon like bleached skeletons of some huge creature -and it looked strikingly similar to the entrance of The Nightmare at Broad River. My heart sank thinking I may have just paddled a long and difficult circle. I stopped and strained my eyes to see some difference. In fact the layout was different. This was not the same lagoon. Then it dawned on me. I was looking at the remains of a destructive hurricane, probably the same hurricane that cleared the swamp forest at the mouth of The Nightmare. Sometime in the past, a tornado swirled down from the sky and laid waste this part of the flooded forest.

I stopped paddling and waited. Slowly I got a sense of a current wide, indirect and hard to explain. I guessed it was the tide receding from the expanse of the Everglades. As I paddled along the current, a creek became more established and then miraculously transformed into a small river. My confidence grew that I was on the right path. The only way to make reasonably sure under these conditions was to confirm every bend and twist to the map and that meant counting turns. I put a dot on the map where Left Creek began and counted from memory the turns I had already passed through.

I came to a large fallen tree blocking the river. Water siphoned under it and lapped over it making the trunk bob up and down. I back-paddled to keep the kayak from being pushed broadside where the current could roll me under.

I looked around. There were only mangroves on either side, no real ground and no portage. I paddled the kayak straight over the log until it beached on top. Then, gingerly, I slid off the boat and straddled the log as if it were a horse. The log was actually floating and with my added weight, I sank chest deep. "Please don't let there be an alligator under this", I said out loud. I would have freaked out had a catfish squirmed underneath me. The log lifted and sank like a carousel horse and when it sank, the kayak slid over. I snatched the bow rope as it went by and deftly tied it to the stub of a broken branch.

The kayak came to a stop calmly pulling this-way-and-that in the current. It made me proud; the graceful way my boat performed, so respectful of its surroundings. It was like a forest monk intimate with the world.

And then the tie-off branch snapped and the kayak started downstream. I caught the rope quickly in the nail-biting last second and pulled the boat back again. I pulled it all the way back to where I could get a real good grip on it. When the log bobbed up high, I slithered onto the stern, shimmied over the green dry bag and back in the seat and plop! Back in the saddle!

I snapped the paddles together, pulled in the stern line and I was off.

Within minutes the river diminished to the familiar collection of mangrove limbos and ponds. Each time I entered a pond I saw what seemed to be two or three exits. The Nightmare was now a puzzle. I could feel doubt at the edges of my thoughts and this was not a good place for doubt. I turned around to see where I'd come. It was as if the mangroves had filled in behind me. What an astoundingly bad place to get lost, I couldn't imagine how I would backtrack in this mess had it become necessary. Forward and through was the only direction now.

Returning to my artist-in-residency at the resort on the Big Island. There was a day when friend and I went to explore the *Center of the Earth*, a lava cave that led down to a cavern where seawater filled a hot pool. It sounded inviting.

But that's not how it turned out.

As we descended into the Earth we moved through a string of domes each with many openings, like we were caving through hollow turtle shells, each one with about five possible exits. Along the way we noticed candles in the black lava gravel that I imagined were used for some sort of native Hawaiian ritual. When we finally came to the hot pool at the bottom, my companion became agitated.

"I got the fear!" he yelled, panicked and bolted for the exit kicking rocks and scree behind him until he was only a distant echo. Following him was the last thing on my mind. I set my headlamp on the floor of the cave and slowly immersed myself in the delightful steamy, womblike pond. It was exquisite!

When I got out I didn't linger, I headed straight back out to find my claustrophobic pal. That's when I discovered the reason for the candles. Each time I ducked though a passage, I found myself in another dome with three or four exits and at least two of them seemed to be the right one. The candles were meant to be lit to indicate the route. I only got out because I could follow my companions staccato trail of scree and kicked over candles.

I found him in the sunlight-dappled forest sitting on a rock smoking a cigarette.

"I freak out in closed spaces," he said.

A couple days later I woke up in the night with a terrific earache. I had picked up an infection from the hot pool and I was beside myself in pain.

Stephan, the artist colony's ad hoc instructor, trainer and grower(...soon after I arrived it became clear that the artist-in-residency was a cover for the marijuana farm out back) placed me gingerly in the back of the VW minibus and drove me to the clinic in Hilo.

But a lava flow had recently closed the coast road and we had to take the mountain road 3,000 above sea level instead. I begged him to stop several times on that road that day just to pop my ears. The pain was excruciating!

Dr. Belcher, wore a threadbare shirt and a three-day-old stubble. He wheeled in a little compressor, had me lean to one side and proceeded to vacuum my ear by poking it with a hard metal tube. When my screams were heard above the din of the compressor, he stopped.

"Well, that'll do. We can really do some damage in there," he said.

*

I popped out of a mangrove limbo into a deep arena-shaped pool. It was larger than the others and evenly surrounded by floating mangroves.

I saw a wave moving toward me from the other side. I thought I was seeing a tidal pulse. The wave came closer and I had a different thought, it was an alligator under the surface scared up by my sudden appearance, or worse a saltwater crocodile. In the past I was shown how alligators use areas like this to ambush prey and I had a strong feeling this was not a good place to be.

The wake pushed forward becoming a series of convex waves disturbing the still, brown water. As it reached the mangroves, the branches shuddered. There was only one place that thing was going: straight at me. I didn't know what else to do but hold my paddle up like a spear and try no to think.

The bow rose, then the boat, and then I plopped down like a ride on a baby roller coaster. Wave number one, wave number two and then three. I waited a moment, I wasn't going to tempt fate. The pond became calm. Whatever it was had gone by, or under. I paddled quickly across to the next limbo (*get thee behind me Satan!*).

It was mid-day and the ponds and mangrove-covered creeks went on and on and on. I guessed I had been in The Nightmare for four hours now. I felt more and more that my boat was my savior and protector. I marveled at the way it seemed to know where to go, finding channels and creeks in a mash of mangroves and ponds. And I wondered out loud about the size of the alligator.

"Probably as long as the boat," I said to the swamp then let out a whistle.

Years ago on the Peace River, I was exploring a shallow tributary. At the end I found an alligator sunning itself on the mud, there was no way out but under me and that was exactly where it went, all twelve feet of it rattling the bottom of kayak, DRRRRRRR! It lifted the boat (and me) like I was a blanket flapping in the wind. And now that I compared, I was sure that gator was not big enough to cut a wake the size of the one back in the mangrove pool. That gator had to be much bigger, a beast of nightmares.

I looked at the water surrounding my kayak and got the chills *(I got the fear!)*. I knew it wasn't good for me to think about the monsters lurking below while paddling through all these deep, brown pools. Creaky doors, opaque shower curtains, mirrors with demons and descents down dark basement steps, there were sure to be more scares without me spooking myself.

I began to think The Nightmare had its own way of living up to it's name. The Nightmare manifested differently for each person that traversed it. But The Nightmare itself was just an empty swamp, an unknown series of ponds with a million different experiences.

In *"Duma Key"* Stephen King's novel set in a lonely and haunted island south of Sarasota, antique lawn ornaments come to life. Hopping cement frogs, a galloping carousel horse and a frightful lawn jockey that smilingly waves from different parts of an abandoned resort home; from the window, from the porch, from the coconut grove...from the bottom of a green cistern...

The route thinned to a small creek with a good current. I reviewed my count of turns and twists. But here the map wasn't very useful; the series of mangrove ponds I had just passed through for the better part of an hour was translated on the map as the thin line of a creek. A creek it was not. I could only guess (and I didn't feel comfortable with all guessing) that I had come far enough to be near an important creek I had to turn into, this time on the right, according to the map it would cut directly 90 degrees off the route I was on now.

Then there it was, the tiniest creek yet, just enough water to make a white sandy delta. Again the mouth was too shallow to paddle through. I got out and pulled my boat over. It felt good to stand up. Every time I stood up in this part of The Nightmare, I felt as tall as a mythological giant in a Lilliputian swamp.

I could see the creek going straight into the forest at 90 degrees as the map indicated. This had to be it. I put a red dot on the map.

Next the map indicated to look for a turn into a creek about five hundred feet ahead on the right. If I found it, I would know where I was.

In the meantime, doubt lingered on the edges of my thoughts. I wondered if the tide had already begun to abandon The Nightmare. If so, did I have the option to take a channel out to the coast? I looked at the map again. Yes, in fact there were several exits I hadn't noticed before. I counted at least four coastal tributaries that met up with this part of The Nightmare and each one was a direct channel to the western shore, one every half-mile or so. I laughed.

Five Hundred Foot Creek appeared. I turned into it. It morphed into a proper, kayak creek as inviting as an amusement park jungle ride full of zigzags and craggy old trees. It widened for a short stretch then withered to a trickle I could barely paddle.

Days ago, when I worked out this route on the map, I had hopes that this area would be good for fossil hunting. But now as I patted the bottom, there was nothing but sand on a soft pile of black leaves that let out a plume of dark mud when I disturbed it. Any fossilized bones would have sunk deep, deep below this muck. I could forget fossil hunting.

Florida is actually a very good place to find fossils, primarily from the Miocene: Mammoth, Saber Tooth tiger, the giant shark Magalodon, basically all Ice Age creatures. I have heaps of Mastodon chunks strewn about my art studio that I virtually kicked up wading down the Peace River. Florida's sandy soil make fossil hunting easy. I heard a story about an RV camp where people had used an outcrop of stone for cooking fires. One day a paleontologist happened to be camping on that site and noticed the craggy line in the stone. He got out his folding camper's shovel and unearthed the complete skull of a Mastodon, ten-foot tusks and all.

*

The tiny channel turned and turned until I felt like I was paddling in a circle. Through the bramble of mangrove, I could see where I had just come from. There was only one spot on the map that indicated this horseshoe. I put another red dot on the spot.

The creek straightened out. On either side were very obvious piles of soil, sand and shells. This part of The Nightmare was clearly dredged, and from the looks of it a long time ago.

It might have been cut in the late 1940's when the Everglades had became a national park or the work of Seminoles, Miccosukee, or Calusa. Maybe I was looking at Tequesta engineering, paddling a canal dug centuries ago long before the carving up of the Everglades into a series of canals regulated by the dyke around Lake Okeechobee.

South Florida's waterways have been completely re-plumbed since the start of the twentieth century. In the original hydrology of the pre-Columbian era, it was said it was possible to paddle a cypress boat from Biscayne Bay on the east coast up the Miami River then through the Everglades and out to the Gulf of Mexico. I had to believe that some of that paddling had to have been down dredged canals like this one.

Then it just seemed so unlikely. How could this construction survive centuries of storms? But they did, didn't they? The shell mounds that the Thompson and Darwin homesteads were built on survived hundreds of storms. They survived because miles and miles of mangroves and ponds absorbed the impact of a mad Hurricane sea, reducing the storm surge to a gentle rise.

*

While I daydreamed, the creek edged right and became deeper. I arrived at a confluence that transformed The Nightmare into a small pond with creeks leading east and west. This was the last exit to the coast. But I wasn't going to the coast. Instead, I turned east, upstream and back into The Nightmare.

79

Almost without thinking, I slowed down when I found a deep pool to clean the mud off the boat. I scooped water with my paddle aiming it towards the bow and watched a satisfying heap of cobwebs, sticks and mud stream off. On the second scoop the paddle skipped awkwardly, I lost my balance and nearly went over. My heart jumped through my throat. It could happen that fast – a crisis and for such a stupid reason.

I paddled on forcefully to vanquish the jitters. There were so many ways one could screw up and they often occurred before you knew it: a minor injury at home becomes infected on the trail, a decision to follow a creek to sends you into a maze to nowhere, that extra water jug you decided was too heavy to carry and left behind. These were the errors that caused the maze to thicken, the web to tighten, the heart to beat faster and The Nightmare to become your own.

Survivalists study the unfortunate situations of people who were lost in the wild. They deconstruct, they backtrack and look for the slip, the bad choice, the extra map, the knife, the string or the forgotten flare gun. It often happens in a team when one person expects the other to bring something (*"I thought you had it!"* -sound familiar?) Our minds are not designed well to prepare for "the point of no return". It takes effort to imagine the fix we might find ourselves in two or three days from now. And more and more our lives have nothing to do with the woods. More and more we enter as bumbling foreigners.

I was quite aware of this and rehearsed *what if* exercises. But no matter how much planning is done, the unexpected happens: the weather takes a turn, boats tip, important tools slid off the deck and splash into the swamp *(or the wind blows the map away).* I was once shaving on the bank of a river when the razor cartridge popped off and fell into the fast moving, muddy water. I had shaved exactly one-half of my face: the right side. I never found the razor and lived with a half beard for a week...and drove home like that.

Maps can be misinterpreted even by the most experienced orienteer and sometimes the map is too vague, the letters naming rivers cover important creeks or sometimes the cartographer has made an out-and-out mistake. It's not very serious if you're in a powerboat or car but when you're slowly crossing miles hiking or paddling, mapping errors can be serious trouble.

That's why you take things you'd never think you're going to need like sterile field plastic sheets, needles and thread. You don't expect it, but if something goes terribly wrong, at least you have the option to stitch together your own blood-squirting artery in a bug-infested forest and live to tell the tale. 'Maybe I'll stay home' you say? Sorry, most injuries happen at home. I say might as well take your chances with the alligators and the nightmares.

*

According to the map, this river would thin out and become a creek. I would stay in the middle to avoid paddling down a couple of tributaries to nowhere all of which surely had alligators at the end of them.

As the river diminished, I pulled under a really low mangrove where the dry branches cracked and fell into my eyes. When I got clear, I was in a pond as diminutive as a puddle in a city street, but the sand was breathtakingly clean and pure, I could see it percolating. In fact I was not in a pond at all but an active fresh water spring. Throughout Florida fresh water percolates up from the oolitic rock. I lamented finding this now. I would have liked to spend an hour meditating near the magical pool. But the day was passing and I had probably been in The Nightmare six hours, I didn't have time to doddle.

Before moving on, I confirmed my position by taking several hanging mangrove roots and crossing them into a knot. I put a dot on the map with the red marker and scribbled a note: "Fountain of Youth".

*

I had learned to leave "breadcrumbs" when paddling the Everglades.

A few months earlier, kayaking with my girlfriend, Jared, I decided to try an untested route. We were between Long Lake chickee and Hell's Bay chickee and I wanted to show her a pond where I had seen dolphins feeding once before.

The map showed a well established channel on the south side of the pond that led to a string of smaller ponds and at the end of one of them, a small blue line indicated a creek could take us through the mangrove to the west shore of Hell's Bay. If my plan worked, we would follow the route right through the small blue line, come out and paddle around a small mangrove island and there would be the revealed our chickee camp for the night.

If we were lucky, she would get a chance to see dolphins in the wild, paddle a delightful creek, discover some hidden ponds and do a little mangrove limbo ending in finding the warmth and comfort of our romantic chickee in the sunset. I thought it was a pretty neat idea.

But that's not how it went.

To start with the dolphins weren't there. The channel proved to be longer than expected which may have been because it was so straight and dull. The only unique thing about it was a piece of rag caught on a mangrove branch.

At the end of the channel I expected to find three clearly identifiable ponds like gems on a necklace, but there were more like a line of wide and thin passages rather than ponds and I would have said there were four, plus they didn't fit the shape on the map, something wasn't right.

"Do you know where we are?" she asked, the uncertainty must have shown on my face.

"Yeah, basically I do, but I have to scout this pond to be sure, wait right here, OK? ...and don't move, OK? Don't move," my stern tone of voice probably didn't help to calm her.

"I need you to be something like a crossed mangrove root, a rag tied to a branch, the place we are on the map." I bit my tongue.

I saw the nasty micro-expression flash. I just compared her to a rag tied to a branch.

Things were rapidly going from bad to worse.

I dutifully looped the pond finding nothing that looked like a creek. Instead I found a hidden bay and that did seem to be on the map. Ok, I knew where I was. I b-lined back to Jared. She had slumped over.

"You OK?"

"Yeah, just a cramp. Guess I'm getting my period a little early," she sighed.

"Well, I know where we are, the creek we want is in the next pond over..."

She gave a sigh of relief expecting we would be back to the chickee in minutes. She paddled up alongside me and pulled down my running shorts. Her face dropped over me and she began to enjoy my company in a way that was completely unexpected.

I still had the paddles in my hand. My body instantly reacted and in one of the shortest, fastest record breaking times, I came off the side of the kayak into the Everglades. She let out a sigh of pleasure herself. Tension was released for the both of us.

"What inspired you to do that...here in the swamp?" I asked.

"I was so impressed that you could find your way that I was in love with you –*at that moment*," she said emphasizing the last bit as a moment subject to expiration just as quickly. "The stink of Zen" I thought, people obsessed with the Buddhist meme "stay in the moment," ugh. I hoped it didn't show on my face. I looked off like a scout in a movie to cover it up.

"Let's go!" I said like Batman to Robin and we hurried off to the next pond.

"Please, wait here, no point in you wasting your energy with me going back and forth looking for the creek," I said.

"Like a rag on a branch," she said.

I was glad to be alone, I didn't want her to see how uncertain I was poking around in the mangroves on the edge of the pond.

The sun was going down, my mind was full of doubt and Jared was losing energy by the minute.

The pond was bigger than the others -that checked. I paddled straight to where the creek was expected to be.

What I found was a tiny, thin channel festooned with mangrove roots covered in spider webs, I couldn't imagine forcing Jared to go through it. I myself was unsure if I was correct and if we ended up stuck there and had to back out, she would break-up with me for sure. I would have broken-up with me.

Uncertainty flooded my mind. What should I do? I sat immobilized in my kayak. Lost. Not lost but lost for an answer. A decision. I paddled back to Jared.

She wasn't there. I was sure I had returned to the place where I left her. Pure panic filled my chest.

I called out and found her just around an island of mangroves.

I laid into her.

"What the hell are you doing?!" "*I told you NOT to move!*" "Don't you understand how important that is in this situation? Never move! *Never Move!*"

I wished I could have taken it all back. I wish I didn't use the phrase 'this situation'. What situation? We're now in a situation? Oh God! Bad Mark, bad boy!

"I got frightened! I don't know who you are. How do I know you're not a guy that invites girls on a wilderness trip and abandons them for kicks!"

"What? What would be the point of that? No way, c'mon." I said, but I got the sense the damage was done. I was not surprised she was losing confidence in me.

"Listen to me, I know where we are, I found the creek, but it was so shallow and dark and the tide may be out and, well, its just not going to be possible. We'll go back the way we came."

"Well, let's get started, its getting late and I have to pee." She said, rallying to the goal.

The way back became a whole new challenge. Normally if you're planning to return the same way you came, the rule is you look behind you every now and familiarize with what the landscape looks like coming back. But now even if we had done that, the sun near the horizon and cast long shadows that rendered even the most obvious landmarks sculpturally different. We might as well have been dropped into the Amazon.

I began to doubt myself and Jared probably felt the same. As we paddled she pointed to every channel and creek we passed.
"I think we came that way," she would say.

I was looking for one thing: that piece of rag on the mangrove root. I focused my mind on finding that one object. Zen practice took over and I felt calm. I looked at every little floating speck, every dappled wave and every fluttering leaf. I saw the spider webs and collected reeds on the edge of the river. I saw the clouds and the movements of the birds. I didn't let anything pass me by without investigation.

'This is the way back here," Jared said.

I stopped paddling. Her constant speculation, although well meaning, was shaking my mental picture of the landscape. I took her alongside and looked into her eyes.

"I know this is going to sound extreme but I need complete silence," I began, "I have to meditate on the trail. Things have changed. I have to follow the way back in my mind. I have to follow the trail back in my head as much as what we're actually seeing, maybe more. It's the only way I know. It's the way I've learned. Believe me, its not difficult but I just have to go step-by-step back in my memory without skipping and that means with no interruption. Can you help me with this subtle process?"

She understood and was newly impressed with my confidence. I pulled her up on a bank of dry soil. I told her to relax and have a break.

Meantime, I asked myself what the worst was that could happen here? I knew that we were not far from the chickee. The weather was calm. I realized the danger was mostly in our imaginations. The worst that could happen was that we would be a little inconvenienced.

I tied a rope to her kayak and I towed her. She fell silent.

I stopped talking, but I was not quiet inside. My mind was jumping at everything I could remember, picking up any clue, dismissing anything that would not hold up. I inched along the route analyzing the relationship of every stick and leaf. I started to hear what we had been saying as we passed places in the channel. I was sure I getting near.

As the sun angled low over the mangroves, in a melodramatic circle of light, I saw the rag. And it was right where I expected it to be. I felt good, very good. I praised all that time I spent on a meditation cushion learning how to rise above the mental chatter and to focus on one thing. But I never expected it to be a survival tool.

"This is the right way, I recognize that tree." She said from behind me, and she was right.

"You're right, I remember that tree, too." I wondered if she did recognize the tree or did she see the rag, too.

I began to see a cluster of remembered shapes and then a very tall tree. I paddled around the familiar bend and came out of the channel onto the pond.

"Oh, look! Look! The moon! Look at the moon!" She swooned.

It was just rising over a hammock of trees. We paddled out into the pond. It was a bright Halloween orange globe in a clear, pale blue, sky. All the tension drained out of me, my shoulders loosened. I almost dropped the paddles.

"Waaaaaaaa!" I growled, relieved.

The sight of the silent moonrise was completely recharging. In the wilderness things can turn from dire to sublime in a flash.

I paddled through the switchback to big Long Bay in short order. My energy was tremendous, and I pulled her kayak like I were cracking a whip.

We entered Hell's Bay and there, plain as the rising moon we both spotted the chickee's rectangular lines, a welcome sight in the middle of nature's designs of curves, waves and teardrops. It was no more than a quarter mile away. I could see my colorful dry bags hanging from the beams and my tent, sienna orange.

"Woo hoo! Home!"

I sang a little sea shanty for Jared I was so happy.

The sun had set by the time we tied off at the chickee. Tired and wrung out, I prepared an easy dinner of canned tuna, salmon and crackers.

The night was cooling and I put Jared in the hammock and covered her with a blanket while I cleaned up.

Lying flat on my stomach I leaned over the chickee's wooden deck and rinsed out the cans of tuna and salmon. I stared at my dark reflection.

The water exploded.

I arched away from the splash bending my back and pulling muscles all up and down my torso. I hopped up to a stance and watched an alligator tail move away from the chickee.

"Goddam it! Goddam it! That alligator almost bit off he artist's hand off!"

Jared's panic rebooted. But she was too tired to do much about it. She slid her back around on the hammock and covered herself with the blanket.

I was shocked. I paced the deck staring at the dark shape in the water. In my world, alligators were fairly benign, docile creatures that slept all day and hid underwater when you came near.

"Until they don't," I said to myself.

I watched the alligator circle the chickee, it dragged a yellow nylon rope tied around its upper jaw. Someone had tried to capture it. Now I felt nothing but pity for the creature. Its mouth had been tied shut before it got away and now it was suffering a slow starving death. I considered ways I could cut the yellow cord, if I had a pole long enough maybe I could strap a knife at the end of it...

Then I remembered the wide-open white mouth. It lit up creamy white in my headlamp's LED beam. The mouth was not tied shut. I went to bed at least knowing that the alligator wasn't going hungry.

She circled our chickee for hours haunting us with a threatening growl.

"They can jump, you know," Jared said.

"Those are crocodiles. Crocodiles jump. Gators don't jump," I reassured her, but I wasn't very convincing.

"It jumped at you," she reminded.

Maybe it was a croc. Could I see it well enough to tell? A crocodile could jump right up on the chickee without a second thought.

My back hurt. The reptile had already inflicted an injury. We dozed listening to her growling lullaby. I reassured myself that this water was too brackish/fresh to interest a crocodile. I imagined: a slapstick image: I am being dragged off the chickee while my girlfriend kept on chatting unaware. I cuddled up to Jared and rubbed myself on her nakedness to relieve my stress. I had already transcribed the lost-in-the-Everglades-interlude into a functional sexual fantasy.

The rising sun bathed us in its warm light and made us perfectly blissful. The gator (yes, it was a gator) spent the night nearby. I found it floating motionless by the edge of the mangrove.

A pontoon boat motored up to the chickee. On a giant plastic tank that took up half the boat someone painted "Mr. Stinky". A park ranger dressed in Park Ranger clothes greeted us and got straight to work cleaning out the port-a-potty with a noisy vacuum hose. He said the alligator's name was Snagglepuss and he had been terrorizing overnight campers at Hell's Bay chickee to the point where the park service staff decided to resettle it away from people. But as the yellow rope testified, it was a work in progress.

*

I slipped under a wall of mangroves and proceeded into the longest limbo I would encounter in The Nightmare. I scratched and scraped through it until I gave up thinking what I was doing. If I had encountered this mess any other time I would have given up but here I seemed to be immune to critical thinking. It was like I had taken a pill and become a machine that only went forward. When I found a gap, I straightened up and attempted to clear the bits and pieces of bark out of my eyes. I took the map out from under my seat. It seemed to show I would be in this creek for a full mile. I followed the squiggly blue line up, up, up until I found the printed black letters: BROAD CREEK. I was in Broad Creek. I would have named it Limbo Creek, Skinny Creek, or no creek at all.

Broad Creek never got bigger than a sidewalk. My slim kayak challenged its width. The curves and curls suggested a wild creek. There was a current I could almost describe as babbling and the water was clear and free of leaves. The bottom was sand and at times the kayak skidded over it with a meditative *hissssss*.

This was obviously the area that marooned you at low tide.

I wouldn't mind if I did have to camp here for the night. There was a nice spacing between the trees perfect for the jungle hammock and plenty dry ground. With a bag of food and camp stove and candles, I could be very comfortable here.

I marveled at the tiny pools and swirls, terrariums and aquariums. I passed small fish and an occasional turtle, frogs leapt from the bank, and water spiders raced along the surface. Broad Creek's miniature charm was utterly mesmerizing.

There was a subtle change in light, the sun had begun to lean into its descent and the dappled light vanished from the forest floor. Now a golden shimmer reflected off the green, leafy treetops. The day was passing and I had a third of The Nightmare to complete before I got to the chickee.

The first tributary of Broad Creek appeared on the left. It was a surprise and reminded me not get caught up in the spell. I poured over the map and found the tributary. It was partially covered by the giant "C" in the lettering of *Broad Creek*. The winding line that represented sideways creek went steadily nowhere for over a mile before it came to a dead end. Another trap.

I started to count the small bends in the creek- right, left, right, left. If I counted them accurately I should be able to predict the confluence of the next tributary.

I marked the map with a red dot for every bend in the creek. I was amazing at the detail of the map here. I felt like I was watching myself from high above moving through the map/landscape. After twelve turns to the right and thirteen to the left, Creek Number Two appeared just where it was expected.

Here Broad Creek would become wider and I calculated that 700 feet ahead I would find a confluence of several channels filling a pond.

Instead the creek opened up into a wide channel and curled back to the west. This was not what I expected. I set the paddles down to study the map with a magnifying glass connected to the compass. The kayak came to peaceful stop on the roots of a mangrove.

The bend made sense if I was farther along. The map indicated I would find a creek not far ahead on the left, if I found it I would know where I was.

I paddled close to the bank and found Know Creek. It was nearly invisible under a wall of low hanging mangrove branches, but it was there just the same and right where it was supposed to be. I was back on the map. I reset my mental map and put a red-dot on the spot (but qualified it with a question mark just to be safe).

The sun had sunk close to the horizon and it was getting hard to see the details of the map.

"Headlamp. Headlamp," I said to myself. But there wouldn't be one, it was stowed far too deep in my clothes bag and there was no shore to beach and dig it out.

"Keep it up front," I thought.

I studied the map with the light available and tried to memorize the way to the chickee. The route was easy: follow this river straight southwest, with a few changes more or less. Easy.

I passed a creek on my right, the river opened up to the setting sun and it lit the wall of mangroves in an orange-yellow light. It reminded me of church calendars and jigsaw puzzles, of scenes of cookie-tin New England towns resplendent in fall colors.

The creek was a landmark that I had to pay attention to. Next I was to look for a channel on the left in 400 feet and take that.

I found it hidden by trees, only when I looked behind me did I see it. You had to know it was there.

"Stay focused, paddler," I counseled myself, "steady…as she goes…The Nightmare may still have some tricks".

With the last strains of available light topping the trees I paddled the home stretch.

I speculated what would have happened had I missed the channel; I would have made it to the Harney River but would have been surprised to find no chickee.

Maybe I would have panicked and that's a wild card, any amount of speculation can get tossed out. But, if I figured out my mistake I could have turned and paddled upstream for fifteen minutes and found the chickee anyway. If I had chosen to go downstream, I would have paddled to the Gulf of Mexico (using the light of dusk) where I would have probably made camp on the beach in full darkness to work things out in the morning. It actually may have been quite interesting.

Daylight was rapidly slipping away. I raced through the final stretch, the calm water offered no resistance and I glided over the water like a low flying pelican.

I came around the last oxbow and found the chickee on a cork island as I arrived at the Harney River.

"Helloooo!" I crooned, jubilant. Out of The Nightmare without a hitch!

Harney River chickee had to be the tiniest, oldest and most dour chickee yet. The whole dreary thing leaned like a drunken man against the mangroves including the port-a-potty. It looked like a spooky cartoon.

I dipped my paddle and brought the kayak alongside the dock.

The chickee creaked as I put my weight on it. It was nothing like the sturdy structures I had camped on so far. I wondered if the fallen trees across the creek earlier in the day and this rickety chickee had something in common: Hurricane.

I had completed The Nightmare flawlessly but with not a lot of time left over. I unpacked only what I needed wearing an uncontrollable grin. I pitched my tent as the platform shifted and creaked under me.

I made some hot tea and settled for crackers and sardines, and whatever else I could find that didn't need a lot of cleanup. I was craving sleep. I could feel it like the subtle waves of the returning tide, unstoppable.

While I ate I reviewed the day in The Nightmare like I had just sat down to a slide show. Expecting something frightful, the creeks and channels didn't live up to a horror story at all. Expectation is hard to live up to in any case, I thought. To be surprised was always better.

Perhaps the real nightmare was yet to come. The nightmare I would have tonight that replayed all the possible horrific outcomes: That log I had to jump on: It sinks deep in the water, the kayak gets way from me as I reach for the rope. I am left alone with only a t-shirt and running shorts. Mosquitoes and no-see-ums come out and drain my blood.

What about snakes? Weren't there snakes in the mangroves, there must be a few venomous Everglades snakes, aren't there? (Yes, there are! Several rattle snakes and a nasty coral snake, though they prefer terra firma).

And what about the deadly spider or two skulking within inches of me somewhere along the route? I had heaps of them running around on me, their spindly legs darting about in that staccato manner. There was no chance to identify the Brown Recluse or a Black Widow in the mêlée (both make the Everglades home).

What would have happened if I took the troll's advice and paddled up Wood Creek right out of the gate and did five miles of mangrove limbo before the creek concluded into a muddy pool?

What about that pond full of alligators? And that huge thing that made the wake in a pond impossible to escape from? It went right underneath me. Looking back on it now, it was the stuff of teeth-chattering terror.

Perhaps that was the real nightmare. Like a tale from Lovecraft's imagination, the creeks and channels embedded a hypnotic suggestion to crave sleep, a sleep filled with all the places you could have fucked up, drowned or been eaten in, Your body caught under a serene bramble of mangrove roots deep in brown water, a cold pasty hand slowly waving in the current.

I heard a splash coming from around the bend. I jumped like a spooked deer. I scanned the river for an osprey or a dolphin. What I saw blew my mind. A headlamp darted here and there reflecting on the water. It was a man in a canoe! He had obviously just made it through The Nightmare. What's more it was instantly obvious that there was no place else for him to go.

I started making room.

"Ahoy! Canoe pilot!" he pulled off his headlamp and I could see a look of relief on his face. Somehow we would both have to fit on (and not collapse) this 10x10' piece of wreckage.

His name was Jim, he was from the Northeast and he was cool. Or he was a phantom cooked up by The Nightmare. A person that's existence or non-existence was not clear. Maybe Conrad's *"Secret Sharer"* had just arrived. I wouldn't have doubted the possibility.

He quietly worked with the area he had.

"Don't worry, I'll take as little room as possible. I really appreciate it. I got so stuck in The Nightmare, the last hour or so. I planned to make it to Shark River chickee tonight..."

"No problem, but Shark River's a long way, I doubt you could have made it all in one day." I said trying to put his gratitude back in his pocket before it got embarrassing. There wasn't enough space on the chickee for that.

"Yeah, your right. It is a stretch...but I had days in the Allagash this summer with stretches as long. Never can trust the map."

"The Allagash Waterway?" The Allagash is a series of creeks and rivers strung together in Maine's north woods and considered to be one of the most beautiful paddling experiences in the country. Thoreau paddled it in 1857, and there's an apocryphal story of two campers in 1976 being abducted by aliens in a flying saucer in the Allagash. Paranormal stardom, that's real credentials.

"Well, you're short five hours of daylight in an Everglades winter compared to a summer paddle in the Allagash. I'd say you did good." I complimented.

Jim was not adding feathers to his cap. I could see he, like me, was hooked on letting the day go by paddling silently from one spot in the forest to the other.

"Most of my trips have been right here in the 'glades, but I did Boundary Waters and the Manistique in the Upper Peninsula of Michigan, that was a good one."

I started preparing for bedtime, "hey sorry, don't think I'm anti-social, but this is a meditation trip for me so I'm just going to slip into my tent and sit for a while before bed."

"Oh really, I do a bit of that myself. There's a Tibetan Buddhist monastery in Maine, I go sometimes."

"I heard about that one." I said.

Jim was a kindred spirit. My meditation only benefitted by having him in the next tent, no different than being on a meditation retreat, elbow to elbow, kneecap to kneecap with other meditating Zen students for fourteen hours a day.

When I woke, his tent was already down and he was almost finished loading his canoe. I just got out of my tent in time to see him off.

I reached for my camera as he paddled away in a river as flat as glass. He set his paddle down turned and waved goodbye, it was the only picture I had of another person on the Waterway and it was perfect: A man in a canoe surrounded in a morning of steely blue, a tiny wake extending from the bow of the boat, an undercurrent of serenity that nourished the entire journey.

*

I left Harney River chickee with a light heart headed for Canepatch where I planned to stay for two nights. It would be my meditation retreat in the wilderness, my days of serenity. I would trade my paddles and map for my meditation cushion and bells.

Canepatch campsite has the unusual distinction of being listed on the National Historical Registry. The site has been occupied for several hundred years and possibly much longer. Fruit trees and sugarcane grow there that still produce fruit. Some guide books mentioned mango trees but I saw no hint of that, and at any rate mango season was in June not January. It's praised as one of he best sites along the Wilderness Waterway and the only substantial piece of land on the route, and being twenty miles inland, I thought there might be fresh water.

The same river I photographed Jim paddle an hour ago, was now a harsh reflecting pool of overexposed morning sunlight. It was a wide and slow moving river that offered little change in scenery. Though I paddled vigorously, I felt as if I was barely moving. A half-mile from the chickee, I left the Harney and entered the North Harney River. The map showed it thinning out before returning to the Harney and I hoped I would find it more pleasant.

I stopped along the bank to rub on some sunblock and refill my mug. The dull overexposed scenery was activating my caffeine monkey and this morning I was guzzling.

The tea mug sat in a cup holder between my legs and wore a red fez, an improvised plastic cup that kept the paddle water out. Another tin cup bounced around by my feet. That was 'the kayakers friend'. Chances to stand and unzip were few. I kept an extra pair of paddles tied on top within reach. I've been schooled. Too many times I've had paddles break at the wrong time. Once crossing a shipping channel, my paddles broke perfectly in two just as a humongous Maersk container vessel bore down on me at 20 knots. Talk about panic!

I prefer wood paddles to aluminum and I believe the extra money is worth it. On long trips day was spent looking at the paddles. Watching them rise above in the sky, making the blade cut the water just right to turn. The dig in, feeling the weight, hearing the hollowing sound, the arc of water cascading off the varnished wood shimmering like diamonds in the sun. Watching them arch across as the turkey vultures glide this-way-and-that in lazy figure 8's. Clouds slowly forming in the morning sun as the shining paddles lifted and turned, a slight wobble as they slide into water, left, right, left, right. The golden amber paddles, the beautiful paddles...

The North Harney continued nearly as wide as the Harney River for a mile or more before it finally thinned out. Along the way I passed one, two, three creeks. I drifted for a moment to study the map. It showed these creeks twisting, turning and intersecting in the mangrove landscape. They seemed to have no possible reason for being. They were like the puzzles found in the last page of a newspaper. I let the kayak drift and came about as I followed the lines solving the mazes from start to finish several times. I was difficult to pass them. I could hear the siren call from the labyrinths. I wish I could have spent the day exploring that area.

Just about every day there were seductive lagoons, creeks and coves I wished I could have spent the day exploring. The Wilderness Waterway could easily be expanded to a 3-month trip that would have been unforgettable. I envied the Calusa, in the way one envies people who lived in a world with less than a billion people, before the industrial revolution hockey-sticked the population to today's 7.5 billion in a few hundred years. In half my lifetime the human population had doubled. I envied with selective nostalgia those ancestors who lived where wilderness was just outside the village or around a bend in the river. Where the road ended and the hunting trail brought you out to the realm of animals. Where nature ran itself and there was no needed for maintenance, no need for public outcry for protection.

*

A school of mullet skittered along the surface of the water at the bow interrupting my daydream. One fish flopped into my boat and slapped around by my feet. A bigger fish must have been chasing them making them scatter. I tossed the fish out and returned to paddling.

Ahead was a small creek that wound around playing in the mangroves for a mile before getting back to business on the Harney River at the mouth of Tarpon Bay. As I slipped into it, I was immersed in silence and the feeling of warm, still air on the skin. It was a perfectly clear creek: sundrenched, clean and sparkling. I became blissful, the silence accented by the papery flap of a dragonfly's wings. Fresh, green mangroves spread out on each side, each with it's own painted, leafy highlight. As a bee hovered along the bow of my boat, all my thoughts vanished and time slowed to a stop.

*

In the forest where I grew up, before I started school, my mother would take me on nature walks and show me the lines in the leaves and the ants working and ask me to listen to the wind in the treetops. They were days of innocence, for me and for her. Days to forget the real hell she suffered in the ravages of war and the resulting mental illness, a little girl living in hunger and fear, surrounded by the smell of death coming from Auschwitz only two miles away.

When she died, I stood over her grave and recited the poem that spilled from me hours after I learned the news that she silently perished from the blood disease,

I was swimming in the ocean when you died.

The sun casting diamonds on the sandy bottom.

Below: the shadow of a spindly stick figure,

Ghostly,

Translucent,

Cast upon the half-seen,

Half-guessed,

Un-clarity.

I turned to take a breath.

Gazing out from meditation, clouds passed and

Leaves shuddered in the breeze,

I recalled you gazing at me, deep in that passive,

Snakelike drift to death.

"Where is my Father?" you asked,

I turned my head skyward and inhaled cool, sea air.

Spotted eagle rays wearing clown's faces glided on the sandy bottom,

Sand ribbed from last night's tide.

A fever was the last thing you knew

Turning right to take a breath lifting the heavy,

Cancerous belly.

In Laos, in Luang Prabang I sat like the Buddha in an

Abandoned meditation hall,

A young boy came to show me a singing beetle

He caught with his own small hands,

As the malaria blossomed,

And others gathered mangoes in the forest.

I was swimming in the ocean,

The sun casting diamonds on the sandy bottom.

"Do you mean I am going to die?" you asked.

"Yes," I said.

Just below, I saw the half-shadowed stick figure,

It's tiny cry hardly more than a mirthful siren from the lips of the ocean.

It comes and goes in the translucent halo of salt and sky,

Dancing on Buddha's sandy belly,

The old man said it once, and they wrote in Sanskrit,

And called it Diamond Silk:

"Thus you shall think of this fleeting world,

A star at dawn,

A bubble in a stream,

A flash of lightning in a summer cloud,

A flickering lamp,

A phantom,

A rainbow,

And a dream."

*

The creek curved left and then right, right again and then left. My paddles rose in the blue sky then sank in blue-green stream. Egrets perched on top of the stunted mangroves studied my movements. Far above, a skein of pelicans seemed to slide off the sky toward the Gulf of Mexico and beyond that, a white half moon in the cloudless, hazy powder-blue expanse.

The creek took a tight turn then continued relatively straight. I knew what to expect. I had become a master of map reading. Now each time I referred to it my eyes instantly settled on the spot where my turns had already been tallied. The creek widened and an even wider channel appeared on the left. I paddled into the confluence.

Although the guidebook said to take Avocado Creek to Canepatch, I noticed on the map a spindly line that wiggled up and over to connect with Avocado Creek just north of the campsite. The creek was small but the map did show it passing through. I had time so I decided to take a look.

To get there I navigated the east end of long Tarpon Bay hopping along islands, points and peninsulas and keep the wind mostly on my back. I held the paddles out like a sail, the bow sliding over the choppy water like a skipping rock.

I came to Otter Creek and then to North Prong Otter Creek. Neither of which resembled anything like a creek, an otter or a prong. I would have left them nameless. They were wide, wide channels between islands.

I hugged the southern shore passing a dizzying array of cuts, channels and tributaries that nourished the bays. Then the open water thinned to a cone shape funneling down to where the creek would be. But all I found was a disappointing little spit, just a trickle under a thick mangrove. I pushed into it limbo-style but it didn't open up any better and I soon found myself and my kayak covered in spiders in a forest high and dry without any creek at all.

I suppose it may have been possible to walk it, and I stood up and considered dragging the boat by a rope like Humphrey Bogart in The African Queen. But the kayak drew six inches fully loaded. I wasn't going to make it, not dragging for over a mile. That adventure would have to wait for another day.

I backed out and set my sights on Avocado Creek.

*

I passed by a small island with a brown line of soil. I tied off my kayak for lunch. It was not much more than a muddy bank so I ate sitting on the bow with my feet in the water. I prepared a lunch of sardines in tomato sauce, crumbly cocktail bread, trail mix and a navel orange that was so good it brought me to tears.

I glanced at the clock stored inside the Pelican dry case. It was only 10:30 in the morning. I had the rest of the day to paddle and not much of any creeks left to explore. I became giddy thinking about the fine dinner I would have on the luxurious picnic bench I expected at Canepatch where I could spread out my food like a buffet.

Before I left Lunch Landing, I took out my meditation bell and struck it three times. The clear, cleansing sound peeled across the water, ebbed and vanished into the ongoing Everglades hum.

I packed up and paddled out of Otter Bay and crossed Tarpon Bay taking advantage of a shortcut through an island. It looked like I was paddling through a pile of jigsaw puzzle pieces, all green and all mangrove islands. I crossed some big water to a wide-mouthed channel and around another island. At the mouth, I came left around a small island then followed the north shore where I passed a tributary.

The north and south shores of Tarpon Bay slowly came together and seamlessly, as if I woke up and forgot a dream, I appeared to be in Avocado Creek.

Avocado Creek could have been in the Central Florida's Crystal Springs region. For the first time, I could smell the sweet fragrance of fresh water. The creek was at least six feet deep and below the boat I could see the *halocline*; the psychedelic swirls where fresh water and salt water met. I could see all kinds of details on the bottom, fish and stones and shells and all the roots of lily pads, and it was every bit the color of an avocado: the skin, the creamy, soft fruit and the pit.

Once again I was spellbound by nature, nature in the act of being, nature so powerfully beautiful as to mesmerize whether I was there to bear witness or not. Maybe that was Zen, I thought, nature in the act of being. Maybe that was Zen.

Avocado was straight as a draftsman's line banked by short stubby mangroves and accented with the occasional buttonwood tree, a tree that preferred fresh water.

The distance to Canepatch was short and I could feel the tide pushing me there. I beached on a patch of hard mud to stretch and get a view over the foliage. Just beyond the short, stubby mangroves I looked out over grassland to the horizon. I wanted to stop paddling right then and there and run out into it. But this was sawgrass and even a short trot would have left my legs cut and bleeding.

I was sure if I took a photo none of the beauty would transfer. The magic was in the expanse, the smell, the sound and the feeling of the breeze, the feeling of open space, the feeling of "me" spreading out to the horizon, not just being in the expanse but becoming the expanse. The camera stayed in the Pelican box.

I returned to paddling. And with no bends or curves, my navigator-mind sank to the bottom of Avocado Creek. And so, it was that in silence and a full heart I entered a lagoon where, on the left, a well-built dock sported a post with a brown and white tent symbol.

I had arrived at Canepatch. It felt sacred. It felt like a pilgrimage.

Surrounding the dock were trees, real trees, some twenty feet tall and behind I could see bamboo and banana, citrus and sugar cane.

I nearly levitated out of the kayak and ran down the wood walk to the open dirt and Jamaica grass meadow that would be home, today and all day tomorrow.

I took inventory. There was a fire pit bordered with large stones and a rusty metal grill. But oh, look at this! A picnic bench, the luxury! What good deed had I done to deserve this?

I planned out my camp: the meditation cushion under the banana grove, the tent nearby on a patch of flat soil, the entry on the soft grass.

I was jubilant! Canepatch was all the guidebook said it was, and more. No guidebook writes things like: 'It will make you feel like an eight year old!' 'One breath of this air makes you invincible!' 'Serenity is spoken by the wind in the trees!' but it would not be wrong to say so.

Later I looked at my photos of Canepatch, it seemed to have nothing going for it, nothing but a worn out patch of dry dirt without much shade. But it was the only sizeable piece of dirt for miles.

I took all the heavy dry bags out of my kayak and pulled the boat out of the water. It bounced on the dock like a toy.

On the far side of the lagoon, I noticed one very large alligator taking the sun.

"Hellooooo," I called out. The alligator did nothing. They rarely did.

As I turned back to my campsite, I heard the unmistakable sound of an idling boat engine. My head bobbed up like a spooked deer. Did it come from far off Tarpon Bay? Otter Bay? Did the sound skip off the water all the way from Shark River?

A large white Fiberglas boat hull emerged from behind the trees and entered the lagoon. In no time it came alongside the dock. It seemed impossible that a boat this size could get down Avocado Creek.

My short-lived solitude was over. I had guests! I went out to say hello. My mind raced speculating whether they planned to stay the night. If so, tomorrow I might still have the place to myself. Meditation day would still be on. And there was a chance they'd only come to fish the lagoon. I had to know. The closer I got, the bigger the boat became. It looked gigantic!

"Hey, how's it going?" I said waving like a wave, slowly up and down.

The man looked in the neighborhood of sixty and vaguely resembled Earnest Hemingway if you picked the right photo. He stood squarely on the deck like he had been on boats his whole life. My guess was he came from Marco Island, the closest town of any size in the western Everglades and where the marinas had facilities to keep a boat as clean as this one.

"Ah yeah, good. You got Canepatch tonight?" a roundabout question gauging if I wouldn't mind neighbors.

"Yeah."

"Ah, yeah, listen mind if my buddy uses the port-a-potty?"

"Go, please, don't even ask, I just arrived," I said trying not to say anything declaratively territorial.

We talked for a while and I discovered in him another kindred spirit that was just beyond his paddling days. We were both very well relaxed. I liked this guy and would have been happy if they stayed, maybe even had fresh grilled fish for dinner.

There were two other people in the boat who just threw lines out, they didn't seem to care if I was there or not.

"Beer?" he offered.

"Wow, ah, normally I would but this trip, I'm a, I'm on a meditation retreat." I said wondering whether this might grate on his beliefs. Religions had an ironic way of instantly unpacking opinions and creating barriers.

You just never knew and it was often better to keep your mouth shut.

"Yeah," he said looking off into the sky, "yeah, I do some of that…"

"Well, we're gonna move on. Just came for the toilet,"

He seemed to be a contemplative soul himself, deeply spiritual. Or it was as I had sensed earlier, that this far up in the Everglades, fools are few and far between.

I eyed his low-lying back deck and ladder that dipped into the water.

"Say, may I use your ladder to get in and have a quick bath? The deck is pretty high, the bank is muddy and there's that guy over there…" I pointed to the big alligator on the other side of the lagoon.

"Sure," he said, "but that old boy won't do anything anyhow."

I took my bath feeling slightly ridiculous and then forgot about using the ladder and just climbed up on the muddy bank.

The bathroom breaker returned. He seemed like he might have been sick. His face was as white as uncooked bread dough.

I stood on the deck as the boat moved into the lagoon and gurgled further up Avocado Creek and out of sight. I stood there listening to the sound until I could no longer differentiate it from the ambience of Canepatch.

In a way, I was sorry to see them go (even though earlier I was nearly praying that I had Canepatch to myself). My gut told me those fellows would have been good company. But as it turned out I did have Canepatch to myself and the meditation retreat lasted two days.

Notes from the sketchbook dated 2/2/2000

"At Canepatch, I sit all day in meditation. The sky is overcast but for an hour in the afternoon. No one had come by at all. I could hear the alligator's low "growl", it appeared in the evening. It floated about 40 feet from dock, its eyes and nostrils the only thing showing.

Later, perhaps a half hour later, it slowly moved propelled by its tail. I could see now it was maybe twelve feet in length. It came right up to the dock where I stood and we looked at each other for some time. I suppose this was how it got a few meals of de-filleted fish but I had none to give.

Quietly he sunk into the swamp and was seen no more that night.

I recalled the moment in The Nightmare when one of the creatures displaced water as it came toward me down a narrow passage and under my boat that bobbed on the wake."

*

I was up and out of my tent as the sun rose. I boiled water, made tea and assembled my meditation seat on the dewy ground. I laid out a sheet of plastic and added my rolled up foam bed cushion for a zafu, a seat.

I placed a silk sarong nearby to wrap up in if the bugs were getting too distracting. Then I placed the bells on top of the Pelican dry case: one small gong that sat on its own pillow I rang three times at the beginning of each session and before and after a short chant, the other a high-pitched hand-held bell I rang three times at the start of meditation and at the end. Finally, I set the alarm clock where I could see it. A normal meditation was forty-five minutes but at Canepatch I had the luxury of stretching a sitting to two or three hours.

I suppose I was an unusual person, I looked forward to meditation retreats. Rather than be excited about parties, if a retreat was on the schedule for the weekend, I was the first guy to say, "Great! A meditation retreat!"

I positioned myself in a half lotus wedging the rubber flip-flops under my knees. I wrapped the sarong around my legs. Placing one hand in front of my chest in prayer position, I mindfully lifted the hammer and rang the gong slowly three times. The sound moved through Canepatch profoundly then thinned to a clean and clear peel and vanished. I chanted:

Araham samma-sambuddho bhagava
Buddham bhagavantam abhivademi.

Svakkhato bhagavata dhammo
Dhammam namassami.

Supatipanno bhagavato sava kasangho
sangham namami.

I rang the gong three times and bowed slowly as the sound reverberated. Silently I lifted the hand-held bell, DING...DING...DING...
I mindfully placed bell and hammer back on the Pelican, straightened my back, lifted my head, placed my left hand in my right, thumbs not quite touching but just close enough to feel the heat radiating and began.
I sat silently for one hour "unpacking" my koan under an open sky.

After one sit I mindfully made breakfast, then moved my cushion under the shade of the banana grove and sat for the remainder of the morning. In between sitting meditations I took fifteen-minute breaks to walk out to the lagoon or explore the perimeter of the Canepatch. As it turned out, a muddy pond and an imposing thicket of bush and sawgrass surrounded the campsite like a hedge. I saw no trails into the fallow cane field, it was not very inviting and probably a haven for snakes.

I took a longer break mid-morning to do my laundry scrubbing the clothes on the dock using a biodegradable soap. My friend the alligator slithered once or twice on the other side of the lagoon unconcerned. I hung my dripping clothes on a line in the sun and then had the joy of gazing at them during meditations. By noon the clothes were as dry as a stick, it almost brought me to tears. Meditation has a way of revealing wonder in the simplest of activities. Years later in a Buddhist monastery in Thailand I experienced an epiphany while washing a t-shirt in a blue bucket.

I prepared lunch on the picnic table: hot chicken and dumplings, applesauce, carrots, cheese and breadsticks. Wow!

Sitting at the table covered by my gear and maps made me feel like I was at a desk job in a cubicle that had suddenly been transported to the wilderness by sci-fi aliens.

I had two koans. One was my own *"What is time?"* Like the breath, it could be unpacked as a meditation point of focus anywhere. Time and time passing and all that it meant was there whether we noticed it or not.

The other koan was one the Roshi gave me, and these were not to be told to anyone. Not for any deep mystical secret society reason, but only because discussing them may dissipate the power they have to transform the mind. Also you might mention it to someone who already had this koan and an expression of recognition might disrupt your effort. Roshi said it would send you down a rabbit hole of speculation about how they solved the koan when you were likely have a different solution anyway.

Koans are not to be intellectually solved. They are not a word game. They are not a riddle. In fact the answer is not important. A non-meditator might think they work like a mantra, repeated at every out-breath, but even this is not hitting the mark.

From the poetry archive:

I sit here in the shade,

With fragments of a snail's shell scattered upon the dry, sun baked soil,

Struggling,

Apparently,

With the humidity,

And heat.

Sitting with legs crossed- Burmese style.

Watching the Monarch butterflies puddle on the white clouds

Teasing me with their cool moisture.

Remember Canepatch?

That bright day in the backwoods?

A cushion under the banana plants?

Your legs covered in Balinese batik?

Remember Yuli?

Gazing out over the rice fields,

Her face shimmering golden in the sun?

Our eyes following a stand of bamboo to the outline of Mount Agung

And into the blue sky beyond?

By the 3 PM sitting, I became cautiously excited that no one was coming to camp at Canepatch tonight. I came to this conclusion while in meditation and entertaining myself with calculations.

Paddling from Harney Creek chickee at a normal cadence, I arrived here by 2 PM even adding a lunch break and a few distractions. Harney and Shark River chickees were the only two places to come from except for the coast. This did not take into account the "Jim Conundrum" –visitors that showed up out of the blue.

If someone showed up in Canepatch tonight, it would have been a disruption. It's hard to be yanked out of a meditation retreat. You're exposed. During a retreat you stick to the schedule and you sink into it. Knowing what comes next means not having to waste any mental energy on planning or thinking about what to do, how to dress what to bring and so on. Instead you have the luxury of "disappearing into the practice".

If someone shows up, I would have to start talking again, put on my *'self'*, my suit, my self-suit. It would be difficult.

The Self in Zen is sometimes called the 'house of pain' or the "Body of Pain". Ajahn Sumedo, an American who became a Thai forest monk said, "Every time I think of my Self, I get depressed." He didn't mean he suffered from depression in the western sense, he meant that the Self was a heavy and bulky thing and was exhausting. It was a drag. Anyone who has spent time in meditation will have experienced the lightness at clarity of shedding this baggage and know exactly what Sumedo meant.

To keep up our personas, our 'self', is a very exhausting and unwieldy activity. Meditation is a practice that is done outside the self, this is why people find it so liberating. Jiun, Roshi, my Roshi, called meditation a 'vacation from the self'.

To have to greet new campers and accommodate them now would be like being on an acid trip and having a church group arrive.

"Hey! Hi, uh, sorry, I've been tripping on mushrooms all day and my head is about to explode. Would you excuse me? I've got to step outside for a moment, but there's ice tea in the fridge, help yourself, I'll be back in a flash!" (I'm quoting an art school professor's greeting on a day I made a surprise visit to his studio. It's worth mentioning that moments later I heard him howling like a wolf from the alley).

In the afternoon I tried to take a nap to rest my back, but it was too hot inside the tent. I returned to my cushion, rang the bell and settled in for another forty-five minute sit, repeating my curious koan. Soon I began to enjoy the afternoon's excessive heat and blinding light.

I watched the day pass from my meditation cushion, the light moved, the shadows, the alligator, the tidewater, the birds and the insects. All moved through the day unconcerned with my presence sitting on a cushion under the wide leaves of a banana. I sat like a stone Buddha. "The Buddha statues are not there to worship, they're instructions," Roshi always said.

During my time in Southeast Asia, I became a person obsessed with Buddha statues.

On my hunt for the perfect Buddha, I learned about the position of the eyes, the lips, whether standing, sitting or lying down. The way the hands were placed, they all had meaning. They were in a way like the Stations of the Cross I learned in catechism class. I became a collector of Buddha images, a man obsessed with finding the most serene eyes, the softest placement of the hand on the palm, the clearest jade and the most beautiful wood grain.

In a small museum in Laos, I discovered an amazing palm-sized jade Buddha sitting in an unremarkable glass case.

It depicted a seated Buddha in jhana on the night of the enlightenment. Carved by a master jade craftsman, the Buddha's half-lidded eyes captured the sunlight and cast a transcendent glow that seemed to speak of serenity and bliss, It was the eighth stage of Jhana, the deep state of meditation attained by tirelessly removing all hindrances from the mind. The Buddha floated on an open lotus flower, the symbol of awakening. The jade shimmered like a clear forest stream and I could see right through the statue.

It hit me like a ton of bricks. In that jade Buddha, I saw a state of meditation I knew from my own experience, a condition I called "glass".

Your body feels transparent, the wind blows right through it, sounds travel through it, light passes through. This is a real sensation. Not something half imagined. And if you're fortunate enough, this state of jhana progresses into increasingly more subtle states of consciousness, you stretch out and feel the world in wider and wider spheres. Your mind spreads out over the landscape seamless, invisible.

 It's a hard condition to maintain, but made easier if there is nothing to cling to. No tasks, no goals, no ego, no possessions, no family, no self. That is why the practice is so negating of the world of things, of opinions and deluding thoughts. Once you get a glimpse into the world "as it is" in those rarefied states of jhana, there's no going back. You will always see you own troubles and ignorance and that of humanity like a father watching a child trying to walk, you see the struggle of the world with compassion and love, because at the very same moment you see someone's suffering or ignorance, you see yourself. The barrier between you and the other has been torn down.

"I see you, builder if this house, and I have knocked your lodge poles to the ground."

These days, I keep only a handful of Buddha statues, the rest I've given away. One that I've kept in my collection is a teak carving from Bali of a Buddha in the diamond position, a full lotus. I keep it because I recognize the face of my Balinese studio assistant Dewa who posed for the carving, and I find it amusing.

*

I felt more settled in Canepatch than any other time on the trip. In meditation I felt more at home than anything I did in my life and I often wondered if I had been a monk in an earlier reincarnation.

Reincarnation. It was a concept I could hardly wrap my head around. I had to drop it whenever it popped up. It was like uncorking the genie's bottle. It sprouted too many fantasies. And in meditation, fantasy was a rabbit hole. There is a long discussion about the Buddha's teaching on reincarnation. In fact the Buddha remained silent on the subject and many scholars make the assertion that he was breaking from this Hindu concept. It only appeared in the Sutras (the Buddhist scriptures) years after Parinibbana (the death of Gautema Buddha) and there is a compelling argument why. The sanga of monks following and practicing meditation with the Buddha in the Deer Park had to be financed in some way, and those financiers were the Brahman caste. In the Hindu cosmology, the Brahmans were closest to Vishnu because of their many lives lived practicing good karma and they did not like the idea of their worldview being scuttled by a revolutionary mendicant. The speculation is that they *inserted* the story of Buddha seeing his many lives into the Sutras the night of his enlightenment while sitting under the bodhi tree. This action may not be so conspiratorial. Perhaps they just couldn't fathom the idea that there was no reincarnation and added it because the Buddha must have forgotten to mention it. Why not? In that same night, the Sutras describe the Buddha meeting the devil and witnessing a rich collection of visions and hallucinatory temptations.

*

I returned again and again to *being*. Being the sounds, being the fragrance, the heat and the breeze. Immersing deeper into Canepatch's impressionist opus. I sat in meditation on the razor's edge between past and future, waiting to hear what the next peep was, the next splash, the next distant call of the osprey, the flutter of sawgrass, the clack-clack of the cane stalks.

In the afternoon I took a break to overhaul my gear. I emptied the kayak and turned it over. The tape was still stuck to the hull since the Lopez Place repair six days ago. Inside, the boat was showroom clean. I opened the dry bags one by one and spread the contents out on the picnic table.

At this point, I had used six my thirteen gallons of water and just less than half of the provisions. The boat was significantly lighter. I inventoried my food, making clusters of breakfast, lunch and dinner. I dropped a few granola bars into the Pelican box bungeed to the top of the bulkhead. Paddling all day, I was probably burning four thousand calories. I was always hungry.

I snapped a picture of all the gear spread out. Canepatch looked like a plane wreck. Every flat surface of the picnic table was covered; empty dry bags of different colors scattered about and turned inside out to dry in the sun, a familiar blue sponge on the tip of the kayak's bow that I used to bail the boat with. Fortunately, I didn't need it and that was good.

I repacked the dry bags and stowed them for the night. The kayak on land doubled as safe storage from animals. It was the perfect device.

After a day of meditation, my mind was working like a well-oiled clock, not a single frivolous thought was entertained.

I made dinner early so I could have four hours of uninterrupted meditation as the sun set. No one came to Canepatch that night. I extended one sit for two hours and really concentrated on my question of time. I steadied myself on the cushion lifted the bell and rang it three times, again that penetrating sound peeled through the wilderness.

Suspending focus on the very point of the experience, I held my mind there. With each breath I repeated the koan. For two hours not a single sound escaped awareness and as the evening sun tipped, I became a glass Buddha, a water Buddha, a reflection Buddha, a wind Buddha. My body melted into the soil and dissipated into the vast sawgrass beyond Canepatch. I sat through sunset, through the cooling air, through the sky turning from blue to white, to gold to pink to purple to gray. My clock beeped signaling the end of the two hours. I reached to turn it off. I held up the bell and struck it three times.

I took a walk around my Canepatch with the flashlight, the one I found under the bed in Chokoloskee. Standing on the dock, the stars reflected in the motionless lagoon. My mind was as clear and reflective as the pond. It had become virtually silent. I watched thoughts like bubbles rise from the bottom of the lagoon/mind. As they reached the surface of my awareness, they vanished in the clear, fragrant air. Everything passed through me. I was like the thin vapor on the surface of the lagoon. As my eyes acclimated, I saw the Milky Way rising like a column. It reflected in the still water and connected to itself in the vast night sky and became a massive celestial ring over and under Canepatch. Again I felt the familiar sense of home I had the day I began practicing meditation and in all the meditations since, an undeniable sense of home in the resonating nature of each and every thing.

From the sketchbook;

I lit candles and made tea while we sat with the night's sky

And watched the newly hatched alligators wade in the shallow stream.

A firefly passed before my eyes cueing the theater of the mind.

I know the curtain of this theater very well,

Though it has long since risen,

Turned to dust and blown away.

The actors have all refused to leave,

They are dusty puppets in a wonder world,

Bedazzled by sparkling, golden light.

Forming whole ideological societies,

They abandon habit for passion.

Choose wonder over will.

Trade hope for belief and back again.

While all of creation listens in viscous awareness,

And waits for the wall to crumble,

We watched as our own forms and those of a million lifetimes

Blend into the golden light,

Of shimmering wanderlings,

Of wide-eyed reptile infants,

Of sparkling absinthe creatures,

Of every thought we ever had,

And ever will have.

We watch as they blended into the golden light

Of a place never before seen.

And launch a lifetime's pilgrimage.

*

In the morning I piled on a double ration of oatmeal, raisins and cashews. I made tea for the day and dragged the kayak to the dock. Loading was easy now. After the overhaul, I had a neat row of trim, tight dry bags that slipped into the kayak as if lubricated. The two bags that were normally tied on top of the stern now vanished into the hold. The kayak looked so clean and sleek in the water I was compelled to snap a picture. To paddle to Canepatch takes a minimum of three days from Flamingo and I hope I never do the trip in a powerboat. It is a camp best arrived at by paddle. Its charm is in its surroundings, the solitude the silence and the innocence and because of that, it remains the most loved camp along the Wilderness Waterway.

I took a final look around for anything I might have left behind then pushed off and paddled out into the lagoon, came about, took a gulp of tea and waved a goodbye to Canepatch. Even though I promised myself another visit, I have not been back in seventeen years. Canepatch remains in my mind like a mythical Brigadoon.

*

The morning sun was behind me and it lit the submarine world of Avocado Creek in gold and green. I was enchanted all over again.

Today's instructions were: find Shark River and follow it downstream to the chickee on the left. That was it.

As I reached the end of Avocado where it widened into Tarpon Bay, I felt the morning winds. I plied the south bank looking for a cut indicated on the map that would take me south. The cut turned out to be quite large. Wide enough to let all the wind through and I had to paddle along the west bank to stay comfortably out of it.

I came to the southern point and looked across the bay to the wide entrance of the Shark. You could draw a straight line from the point down the middle of the river. I stowed my maps under the seat, had a sip of tea and paddled out in a wind blowing unimpeded into long Tarpon Bay. The crossing was only 700 feet but the windblown waves pounded me broadside. I had to tack to keep the kayak's nose head-on in the waves and for the whole stretch the wind whistled in my right ear. As I got into the Shark, I paddled right up to the mangroves on the west bank and found a windbreak.

The river remained over 100 feet wide for two miles. I don't know why they called it Shark River. I would have called it Shark Bay.

Around midday I took a tributary inland and discovered a muddy spit of a beach. A beach! The kayak hissed onto the sand like a happy dog. I took some aspirin (the kayaker's helper) and wiggled my food bag out of the hold.

As I ate, it occurred to me that I would never be here in this little side creek along the Shark River again. Who else might have stopped here for lunch? Would anyone ever sit here again on this hidden beach?

In respect of the fact, I took out my bell and struck it three times. Then I packed up and returned to the wide, wide Shark River.

Naming this river the "Shark" is not without reason. Bull sharks, big bulldog headed beasts, were not uncommon in brackish waters or even fresh water. Records show that bull sharks have been seen and hooked thirty miles in from the ocean in Lake Okeechobee in Central Florida.

I passed two mangrove islands and the river narrowed to a civilized fifty feet. The course turned right becoming an unnaturally straight channel followed by a ninety-degree turn left down another unnaturally straight channel. Each length was the same. On the map it looked like two sides of a square. Then the channel widened to a natural looking river and I was back in the expansive Shark River.

I noticed a cloud in the shape of a carpet roll moving toward me. It was spinning along as if it were a log rolling down a slope. White wisps spun off and evaporated in the blue sky. It rolled over my head at what seemed only fifty feet above. I turned and watched it until it rolled out of sight behind the trees.

I knew what it was. I had studied at the Severe Storms Laboratory in Oklahoma and the Hurricane Center in Miami (before it was destroyed by Hurricane Andrew).

It was a *rolling cloud*, a descriptive name for a cloud normally seen before a thunderstorm. In this case there was no storm. This one seemed to be a rogue and a tiny, whimsical one at that.

Gunboat Island came into view in the middle of the river. The tall mangroves gave it the looming bow of a dreadnought from the Teddy Roosevelt era. The guidebook said to take notice of the mangroves. They were over five hundred years old. In my imagination they were only single-leafed saplings when Ponce De Leon wandered this landscape looking for the fountain of youth. They were the oldest known trees in the Everglades.

I slowed down and let the current take me up to the 'bow' of Gunboat Island then passed along the starboard side. The kayak hooked on a clump of mangrove roots and I let it come to a scratchy stop. I looked into the interior. It was a brown noodle of interwoven mangroves roots, a heap of cockroaches and crabs scurried in the mud. I had little interest in exploring it.

Just behind the island I found a gleaming metal tripod standing high in the water. It was the last thing I expected to see, something right out of science fiction.

It was an NOAA remote weather station. I circled it several times just to be sure it was actually there.

I wasn't more than twenty minutes away from tonight's camp. But between the ancient mangroves of Gunboat and the moonlander weather station, I added at least another forty-five minutes.

Shark River Chickee was on the south bank of a confluence of two rivers, an intersection actually (only in the Everglades it seems did two rivers criss-cross, making a perfect X like this).

Rather than the trend of tucking the chickee into the mangroves this one seemed to be placed in the middle of the channel. I paddled up to the dock and only had time to tie off the kayak when a sports fishing boat came speeding up to the dock.

A man jumped out and trotted directly into the port-a-potty slamming the door with a plastic '*thud!*' I looked at the guide at the wheel. He just shrugged and moved on to chatting. He told me that the Shark River had a worldwide reputation for excellent fishing. He admired my journey, said he had taken it ten years ago.

"...Not that I didn't like it, I loved it. Just never got around to doing it again. Seeing the backwoods like you are now, its special...its different than blazing around at full throttle, I'll tell you that much."

The man came out of the toilet looking calmer. After seeing this behavior several times, it dawned on me that power boating involved a great deal of bladder control, most of it uncomfortable.

I marveled at the speed they were able to shoot off downriver leaving an attractive foamy white wake in the brown water. I would be paddling for three more days. They would be back to Flamingo within the hour. High above, I saw a jet gliding on the approach to Miami International. It would cover the distance in less than five minutes.

The approach from the west into Miami International was over this part of the Everglades. Whenever I flew, I could retrace my trip just looking out the window. Over the years I caught glimpses of Canepatch, Shark River, Tarpon Bay, Hell's Bay and on and on.

As the last whine of the boat's engine vanished, I stripped down to dry in the sun. Sitting all day in brackish water saturated the skin and it took half an hour to feel dry. Toweling alone did little. So I laid face down in the warm sun blissfully eying the deck's evenness. The construction seemed to be perfect, and the swirling colors of the recycled plastic planking suggested a recent renovation. Shark River chickee was almost sterile, and the breeze seemed to clean it even more. I peered between the gaps in the deck. The sunlight sparkled on the velvety brown water below in lazy hypnotizing patterns. I noticed a spoon glowing in the mud and felt empathy for the fellow paddler who lost it.

The map was drying under the pelican box. I reached for it and perched on my elbows to ponder tomorrow's trip to the next chickee (one inch equals one mile). If I drew a straight line, it was only about five miles, but it was through a cluster of ponds, channels and islands that would double the paddling time. Without a pencil handy I wandered the labyrinth on the map with my eyes alone and imagined the turns, bends, shallows and dead ends of each possible path.

*

The next morning was cold, really cold. I donned the same blue waterproof pants and jacket I wore the foggy first day in Chokoloskee Bay. I looked like I was headed for the ski lift.

I slid the kayak into the water, dropped in and left the chickee behind heading SSE into a short, wide channel.

I immediately entered the labyrinth passing through twists and turns then into a tributary where I got into a channel.

After a mile of swirly paddling, the channel split in two. I came to a stop.

The map revealed the right channel was more direct but either choice would have gotten me through. I took the right channel.

I paddled about one thousand feet and found a second fork of no consequence. Again I could have taken either one. Both went around a teardrop island.

I came upon an area of truly misleading channels. The map showed a virtual maze of feeder creeks entering from the west. As long as I kept to the right I would avoid the whole mess. I put a red dot on my map and kept the right bank again and again.

Labyrinths like these always reminded me of how I first discovered that, with a good map, one could make your own paths. Though it was not without trial and error. One "error" happened with my girlfriend in Hell's Bay (we were not actually lost, but...kind of lost). And I think had I been alone on that trip in Hell's Bay, I would have stuck with my plan A: a short cut clearly indicated on the map. I would have muscled through the dimly lit, spider-strewn creek (even if I had to drag the boat) and emerge within spitting distance of the chickee, arriving there a full hour earlier than the backtracking we actually did that night after nearly having a breakdown. On other solo trips I was far, far more lost and stressed than I was that night with her and came out just fine. She did not cause the problem, it didn't matter who it was with me. The problem was that two people confuse each other. One person's speculation is one thing, but two is exponentially worse.

After many ventures into the maze of the western Everglades, I had developed a resilient calmness for paddling mangroves while having little idea where I was. Because I resigned myself to the possibility of spending the night in the swamp, I didn't care what happened. An overnight the labyrinth might have been uncomfortable, but it wouldn't have killed me. Once I accepted the worst-case scenario, I could think rationally and I never ran out the clock and had to bivouac lost in the Everglades. (Though I did on other backwoods trips).

And there were some trips where I spend the entire day in complete confusion.

*

136

A few years after my Wilderness Waterway journey, I was on a three-day trip from the start of Hell's Bay Canoe Trail to Lane Bay chickee.

The route begins at the side of the park road. You launch into a shallow mud puddle from a simple dock in the mangroves and paddle down a wispy, dredged creek that zig-zags so tightly in some places that its necessary to pivot the kayak in unusual ways to squeeze through. But the path is well labeled with over one hundred bright white numbered PVC poles that are hard to miss. It's really more fun than peril. And when the trail ends in a series of bays, getting to the chickees on Pearl Bay or Hell's Bay is just a matter of time for even a mildly experienced paddler.

But that's not what happened to me.

From the sketchbook:

"Tuesday's entrance into Hell's Bay Canoe Trail was not unusual and I was alone at Pearl Bay chickee. [Pearl Bay is a tandem chickee accommodating two parties so sharing is always a possibility.]

Moonrise was spectacular and in the morning the dolphins came very close. Wednesday after following the markers to Hell's Bay chickee, I headed north for Lane Bay chickee. I had no map today for this leg of the trip, but I had done it before and I remember it was not so challenging.

Trouble began after the first channel to another bay and I realized I had greatly simplified the two-mile paddle from Hell's Bay to Lane Bay chickees.

I returned to Hell's Bay in hopes of regaining my bearings and if needed ask to look at the map two people I saw at Hells Bay chickee might have.

Bob and Betty worked for Boston's MBTA (subway) and were also going the same direction, they were happy to help. I drew a copy of their map astonished by my assumption that I could have done this route [without a map]. I thanked them and started again but very soon my simple map was too simple, it didn't include the landmarks and the channels and ponds on either side of the route. You need those to navigate. I waited for Bob and Betty to come by [with the map].

They arrived but being first-timers, they were getting lost even with the map. I convinced them to let me lead with the map and we began by returning to the spot I was sure agreed with the map. Ok, I found where we were. Since I had been lost several times in this maze of mangroves I knew how easily it was to slide from knowing where you are to [being] utterly lost.

The trick is to:

Remain completely concentrated on the map at each change.

Remember all that you passed (where you've come from),

And all to expect (Where you're going).

If at any point the landscape doesn't match the map, resist the temptation to go further to try to regain the trail.

When this happens, you must go back to where the map and your position make sense. Then as you go along, place a dot [on the map] at each point you are sure the map matches the landscape.

Hours of needless, anxious (even life threatening) paddling can be avoided this way.

In the case of Bob, Betty and me, a powerboat showed up. Not surprising, they were lost, too. They offered to zip ahead and make out the layout of the swamp. We waited and chatted. The powerboat returned in five minutes having seen Lane Bay chickee in the distance. They offered to tow [us] through to "Italy Point", which was a major landmark that obscured the view of Lane Bay chickee [it was what I was looking for but I forgot there was one more bay before it].

They threw us a rope and we surfed the channel behind their wake.

For me this was the second time in Hell's Bay and the second time LOST in Hell's Bay. Take heed of the names!

Bob and Betty and I parted ways, I was making up for lost time [they would camp at Long Bay but I was going further] .

I arrived at North River chickee at sunset where a strong wind blew directly at it.. Exhausted, without the energy to make dinner, I was in bed by eight.

Dolphins woke me up in the morning. In the port-a-potty I pulled down the toilet paper and a tree frog jumped out.

On this day I camped at Watson River chickee, where I had camped two years ago on the Wilderness Waterway trip.

I would return to camp on North River chickee the next day and I took the same route back but (as the distance was short) I chose to look into a short cut I had tried the day before without success. It was in a labyrinth northwest of the main route.

I entered the labyrinth through a side channel and found the lagoon where I had gotten disoriented yesterday.

I was not doing this just to have fun. I was doing it to try to understand what happens when you get lost and when the actual moment 'lost' happens to see what can be done about it.

At the very beginning of my experiment, I crossed two mangrove roots together as if I was making a braid. This was an unmistakable marker on the landscape. Mangrove roots do not naturally twist. I placed a red dot on my map. This was the starting line. I paddled on retracing my turns.

I found the creek I wanted to follow yesterday. The map indicated it would take me through to the North River but it turned out to be impassable: shallow and covered in mangroves. So, I chose another creek leading out to another bay to -more or less- the same place.

When I got out in the open, I went around a peninsula looking for the mouth of the other creek: the impassable creek covered in mangroves. I found it not far away. The mouth on this end was open. I paddled in to confirm my concept of how this part of labyrinth was laid out.

But after a short time what I was seeing didn't match the layout on the map. The creek was too large and too winding. It was undeniably different and after studying the map, I couldn't find where I actually was.

I saw some dangling mangrove roots ahead unnaturally twisted together. I pondered how such a thing could have happened, if wind could have done it or some creature, maybe a bird or alligator twisting its tail in the air.

That creature of course was me!

According to my mental map, the roots I twisted only a short time ago, were not supposed to be here, they were supposed to be over there; about eighty yards behind me behind a veil of mangroves. I sat still in my kayak waiting for the map in my brain to reboot. I was so thoroughly confused that I wondered out loud if I had twisted another couple of mangrove roots and then forgot I did it.

I took one more cursory attempt to find that damn little creek. And after returning to the twisted roots again and getting more pissed off because I had not even gotten as far as I got yesterday (confused yet, dear reader? See how easy it is?).

I gave up.

I headed out of the labyrinth the way I came chastened. I returned to the river route and back to camp on the North River chickee where I took comfort in squaring *my shoulders, stamping my feet and pointing to the deck declaring, "I AM HERE".*

*

Finding a way out of an Everglades labyrinth taught me a few good lessons.

I mentioned the importance of concentration. When I practiced this, I believe I had some insights. Insights I may have missed had I not been practicing meditation.

First, a primer on Zen meditation:

Zen is a practice of concentrating the mind on one object, commonly the breath. All meditation practice begins with developing concentration.

Second, once concentration is established, the meditator observes the mind, including all the thoughts that arise as well as the aggregates, the clusters of thoughts. The meditator also observes all the emotions and physical sensations before a thought arises. This is done to gain insight into what influenced the thought or "birthed" the thought. So right away the idea that meditation is escape or drifting or daydreaming couldn't be further from the truth. Meditation is the opposite and it is hard work. Ask anyone who's done a retreat.

The moment I felt the sensation of being lost, I realized I had (just before) made a dramatic swinging movement of my head. That shake alone could have put my mental picture of the labyrinth into a twist. Remember the game *blind man's bluff?* Where you blindfold a player and spin them around and around? Remember how disorienting that was?

I also noticed that as soon as there was doubt about my direction, I lost the mental map, lost it like forgetting a dream. If only one point in my mental map was thrown into doubt, it put everything else into doubt. What you were sure of before was now possibly incorrect. Facts were no longer facts, they were just words strung together that represented nothing.

When I understood that in the context of getting lost, it was an epiphany. I was transformed. I became a believer in the power of positive thinking. For the first time I had a real, tactile experience of the usefulness of remaining positive to a singular goal or idea.

I saw (could even watch the process) how a negative thought could get you lost in the Everglades and how the same negative thinking could get you lost in your day-to-day life. Thinking positive about your goals was fundamental to achieving success. I was once a curmudgeon about the power of positive thinking but no more. Amazing Grace, listen to me: the backwoods motivational speaker! I guess there's always room to grow and change.

Getting back to my mental toolbox for successfully navigating the labyrinths, both inward and outward, I whittled them down to three ingredients.

One: you have to know where you are going. This means having a map and knowing what to expect ahead. A goal. A plan.

Two: You have to know where you've been. This means marking the route already traveled on the map with red dots, looking behind you to remember the landmarks if you need to back track. In life this translates as: Know who you are, checking off your accomplishments.

Three: Remain jovial. Keep a positive mind. Be confident that things will turn out successfully. Think positive. (*"I think I can, I think I can."*) and stay happy with your work and feel good about it.

There's an old story found in many cultures, a traveler meets a guard or a troll guarding a bridge and cannot pass without answering three questions: *Where have you been? Where are you going?* And the third: *Who are you?* The questions are a map for living a life.

*

Halfway through the short cut to Watson River chickee, I passed a small teardrop-shaped pond. I stayed in the channel as it made a lazy long "S" curve then came to two feeder creeks entering from the left. The map indicated to take the second one, a thin creek 800 feet long. The creek ended at a channel heading straight south. When I came to the mouth, I paddled around a small mangrove island. The view opened up and I was back in brown, splashing, windswept Whitewater Bay. I stopped and took in the view from behind some mangroves. Further along the eastern shore I could see the Watson Island chickee protected from the wind by a mangrove island. I pointed the bow and went for it.

From the sketchbook dated 2/4/2000:

Now at Watson River (Chickee) after the shortest day of paddling, only two hours. I lie on the deck in the sun and bake myself dry thinking 'I never have a chance to do this anymore'.

The heat is inviting compared to this morning's clouds and chill that seemed to foretell the arrival of another cold front.

Now I look up from my writing to see the sun glittering colors of the rainbow off a spider's web spread majestically on a mangrove branch, a thin layer of trees that sheltered me from the winds of Whitewater Bay. I recall a few days ago when I noticed a spider on my arm and in the time it took to (lift one paddle into the sky and back down again) I saw it send out a kite-like web-line. It released its grip on my arm and I watched it float away on the breeze until it was out of sight.

That small moment and the entry in my sketchbook inspired this poem written in 2009,

> *While you were sleeping,*

I watched the paddle lift high in brother sky,

Where it caught a tiny silk line connected to a spider,

In the time it took for the paddle to return to the water,

Spider cast the line,

Cut it, and sailed off on the winds.

While you were sleeping,

Water squirts from his mouth,

He rolls on the surface,

And disappears under the boat,

Leaving a single siren call announcing,

A past of dreams.

A present of dreams.

A future of dreams.

While you were sleeping,

The newborn came forth breaking the surface

And filling the air with a salty aroma.

On the shore, holding the breath that no one would recover,

A solitary girl stands in the wind of a thousand lifetimes,

Flower petals flutter past her face golden and crimson in the retiring sun.

"I will take to the air," she said, "on wings of hope and longing,

Come with me and sing of the multitudes, of the 10,000 things."

And as she nestled squarely on the cupped hands of past and future,

In a bird's nest of sea oats, marl and guano,

The sun set the sky alight, and diamonds cascaded off your paddle.

A precious constant pedigreed in the universe of

Coming and going, coming and going,

Repeating a sound that echoed off the distant clouds and into the

Blooming sky, evermore.

While you were sleeping,

      While you were sleeping,

           While you were sleeping.

*

I woke to another cold morning, a cold I didn't notice in my cozy sleeping bag. Just beyond Watson River chickee at the edge of the mangrove the wind pushed up waves on Whitewater Bay.

Separating the mainland from Cape Sable and the Gulf of Mexico, Whitewater Bay lived up to its name. I could see patches of curling waves and chop in the distance. But I wasn't going there today.

Today I was headed to the chickee on Lane Bay through a route that was still hatching in my mind. If I could find an entrance, I could navigate a labyrinth between the two rivers for half the day.

I packed my kayak while the propane cook stove boiled a pot of water for the thermos of tea. It whirred like tiny a jet engine. My sleeping bag hung airing out on a nail. I stuffed the tent into its orange dry bag. I had to be careful with the poles. If they fell through the gaps in the plank flooring, they could be lost forever. Steam blew around the lid of the pot. I filled my thermos and began the meticulously rehearsed packing of the kayak: Drinking water first (five gallons left), canned food, propane tanks. Packed last for easily access: the clothes, the day's food and the first aid kit.

I took another picture of my boat in the sun admiring its design and efficiency. Now only the Pelican case and the spare paddles neatly secured with the Bungee cords remained on top. In with me: tea mug, flip-flops, a water bottle, the empty tin can and the map. In a back pocket on the seat was a tube of sunblock, the compass and a magnifying glass. That was my boat, clean and simple.

I settled into the seat finding the water pleasantly warmer than the air topside.

The map indicated a lagoon just behind the chickee and two creeks on the east side, one went nowhere and the other hooked around and out to Whitewater. I could paddle along Whitewater but instead I decided to avoid the full force of the winds by going through the lagoon.

I came about and nearly sailed away from the chickee. The wind pushed me behind the mangroves where it became eerily calm. The channel angled to the left where a creek took me to the lagoon. It was a wide creek, about forty feet but it was shallow and muddy.

I paddled in. The waters were so still that even time seemed to slow down. As if the mangrove creek was an entrance to a mysterious dimension. Part of a science fiction novel I had become a character in.

The creek separated. This was my cue to enter the lagoon. Ahead, a small island of stubby mangroves lay in the center of the lagoon confirming the map's accuracy. I'm not sure why but I decided to paddle around it even though I didn't need to. I could clearly see the creek I intended to take in plan view on the south side. Maybe I just wanted to confirm my position.

Whatever the reason, I started to circle the lagoon.

As I approached the far side of the island, I was mesmerized to see my boat hover an inch or two above the mud like a pelican flying just above the waves. It was so shallow I could only dip my paddles sideways on the surface. My bow disturbed the mud and turned the water café au lait brown.

Then the kayak scraped bottom and bumped and slowed down.

I was in a mud field. I had to turn around. I put more strength into paddling left but the bow wouldn't come about and I just went in further.

I pushed forward hoping for deeper water ahead but only managed to slip further into the shallow mud. My heart started racing. I dug my paddles deep trying again to push the boat around. A memory surfaced: The park ranger in Chokoloskee showing me my route. There was a point when he hesitated and tapped his pen on the map,

"Few things in the 'glades are more dangerous than mud," he said, "avoid it when you can."

I imagined the park ranger's boat idling towards the bleached bones of a long dead kayaker still holding paddles, a kayak in the middle of a mud field.

"That's – Gonna - Be - Me!" I belted out each word accenting with paddle strokes of mud.

I fell under the spell of panic and lost my senses. I heaved whole paddle loads of mud into the air.

If I stopped here and tried to get out of the kayak, I knew I would sink two feet or more into it. If I got one foot out, the other would go in deeper. People have died waist deep in mud. This was the real quicksand of horror movies. I had to stay in the kayak and I had to paddle it out.

I kept at it. Mud flew past my face, the adrenaline fed the panic the panic fed the adrenaline. I was loosing the battle. The kayak moved slower and slower, a snail's pace. A paddle-clod of mud hit my cheek. I had a glancing memory of throwing dirt on my grandmother's casket in a cold grave in Chicago. I dug my paddle in and pulled hard. I could the feel strain on them. They were not designed for this and were close to snapping in two. I felt some movement, but I had to pull harder, if I lost momentum now, it would all be over and I would be facing a slow death fifty feet behind the Watson River chickee where only moments ago–everything was fine.

The mud tuned darker, more solid, I chucked it with more vigor and I felt a tiny slide then caught bottom again. I leaned forward and dug deep using my paddles like a pole. I felt the muscles in my back and arms tearing away as huge bucket load of mud clunked on the stern of the boat. One -then two -then three! I was moving! I'm sure! I could feel it! Eight maybe ten inches forward with each stroke! *Goddamm it, go!*

The paddles were bending unnaturally.

Remain jovial!

Remain jovial!

I indulged in a prayer for the paddles (*do not fail me, oh, most sacred paddles...*). I felt a little momentum build, I was sure I felt, yes, I was moving! I remembered a nightmare: I was crossing the shipping channel again near my home in a strong current and unnaturally churning and unsettled water as a giant container ship advanced. My paddles broke and fell into the waves beyond my reach.

I cursed the image and chucked it from my mind like the clods of mud thudding on the back of the boat.

"C'mon gagggammit!" I dug my paddle in as far forward as I could reach and pulled one mighty Herculean stroke. "*Aaaaaggghhh!*"

The boat broke over the shelf into a foot of water and slid away.

I paddled like a windmill until I was beyond the tiny island, out of the lagoon and out to the channel in a paradise of deep water.

I stopped, forced myself to stop paddling.

"Stop, stop, easy there, easy…" I gasped, gulping air, I talked to myself like I was a panicked child (which I was). Forced myself to take slow breaths an vanquish the hyperventilation.

The kayak came to a stop in a bramble of mangrove roots. My fingers remained gripped around the paddles I couldn't loosen them. I looked behind me at the lagoon. A brown cloud marked my trail out of the mud field. (The mud field!) Waves of pain spiraled up and down my spine. My kayak was covered in mud. Both on the bow and whole clods piled up on the stern. Finger by finger I loosened my grip and glanced over the paddles for cracks. My arms felt like torn rubber bands, like I had spent the morning playing catch with boulders. I tried to splash water on the kayak then stopped when my arms protested in burning pain.

I moved alongside a bank with a solid shore and got out. My whole body hurt.

I opened up the hatch and rummaged for the first aid kit, got out four aspirin (six) and the Tiger Balm. Swallowed the pills and stripped to my waist rubbing in dollops of balm wherever I could reach. The evaporating camphor made me shiver with chills.

I unceremoniously pushed shovel-sized clods of mud off the stern. A cloud of light brown billowed away in the current. I stood straight up and stretched.

It hurt something awful and I wished the aspirin would hurry up. A floating cloud of mud covered the entire lagoon and now it reached the channel where the current pulled it downstream.

What the hell was I thinking??

I had to use both arms to push the heavy clods of mud off the stern. I caught glance of the other end of the boat as the bow was dipping down into the water. Then it dawn on me. Did the mud on the stern lift the bow enough to make it possible to turn the boat? I remembered how I leaned back in Chokoloskee Bay to bring my submarine kayak's bow up. Did that do it? Of course it did! I laughed out loud. I imagined a cartoon version of myself flailing pounds of mud on the back of the kayak to the sound effect of clanking coconuts.

Then an image of what might have been. I saw myself in the middle of the mud pond with my head down,

153

waiting for the tide but then remembering high tide came in the morning when I entered The Nightmare and that I was in mud lagoon *during* high tide. Higher water would not come. I would have sat there helplessly watching the pond drain even further, my kayak slowly pressing deeper into to the mud becoming glued to it not knowing what to do.

"Few things are more dangerous than mud," the ranger said, "avoid it when you can."

I paddled away feeling comforted by the look of the freshly washed lime green kayak but the mud pond wouldn't let me go.

I analyzed the sequence. Where was the *point of no return*?

Maybe it was my overconfidence. Certainly deciding to paddle the pond when the exit creek in sight was unnecessary. Then I thought about the ham-handed decision to paddle through the mud rather than stop right then and there and back out. That, I decided, was the *point of no return*. When I continued to paddle into the mud, that was when I tipped the odds badly against me.

I took out my red marker and wrote *"MUD!"* in big, bold letters over the pond behind Watson River Chickee. It happened that fast, I thought, it happened within minutes of leaving the comfort of camp.

Returning the way I came I passed Watson River chickee. It wore a poker face, as if nothing had happened behind the mangroves, it looked like a scene from *Deliverance.*

*

As soon as I paddled out into the north end of Whitewater, the wind caught me and pushed me back into the mangroves. I pointed the bow off and paddled away. I could feel the damage I had done to my back and arms. Apparently today was going to be a long, painful one using muscles that should have a healing day of rest.

Once I got a fair distance from the mangroves, I came about and let the wind blow me behind a point on the eastern shoreline.

The route was easy to see on the map, head up the North River to the North River chickee where I could stop for lunch and plan the route to tonight's camp on Lane Bay chickee.

Upstream from the North River chickee, was a channel called "The Cutoff" that linked North River to Robert's River and from there I might find a sinewy line through the massive labyrinth between the Robert's and the Lane River. If I could find a way through, I would go into the labyrinth.

Getting to the North River may have looked easy on the map but in reality it was not. I had to cross a large windy bay followed by an even larger and windier bay where waves broadsided my kayak and sent cold spray into the air. I had to zig-zag to keep the bow pointed to the waves doubling the distance and time. Twice my paddle skipped across the water instead of digging in and my leaning-in nearly sent me overboard.

If you were to zoom out to a satellite view of where I was at that moment, you would see the east side of Whitewater Bay characterized by a cluster of smaller bays leading to rivers, then to creeks and then to tributaries that spread deep into the vast sawgrass meadows of the Everglades. On the map these smaller bays were festooned with a myriad of teardrop and heart-shaped islands. This was one of the best examples of why the area was named the Ten Thousand Islands though I would have called it the Ten Thousand Bays.

I paddled along a thin island that sheltered me from the full brunt of the wind. As I came to the point, I saw waves unimpeded coming from Whitewater. Brown sea foam swirled behind the dead tree branches and gusts blew them into the air.

Getting to the very edge of the mangroves, I pointed my bow at another island in the middle of bay and went for it. Immediately I felt the wind. My back was a sail. I used the paddles as a rudder. Paddling would have been less stable and once I picked up speed I was surfing the waves. I made the quarter mile crossing in a matter of seconds.

With the relative comfort of the island I turned to look back at the uninterrupted view into Whitewater Bay. I could not see the western coastline, the massive barrier island called Cape Sable. The bay seemed altogether vast and wildly un-navigable for a paddler.

In the basic route map for the Wilderness Waterway the instructions are to make a straight crossing North to South of Whitewater Bay for what must have taken a full day. In a kayak, it would have been a battle but in a canoe it would have been dangerous folly. In this wind, a canoe would have either blown into the mangrove shore or capsized.

I passed along the north shore of the island and headed out to open water again, this time to get to a large "C"-shaped island. The wind pushed me across so quickly I felt like I was on an amusement park ride. Once I got behind the mangroves of C Island, the bluster reduced to a light breeze. I set my paddles down on my lap to relax. My arms were aching, my heart pounded in my ears and reminded me of a reoccurring nightmare I had as a child.

My father was seated on the edge of the bed reading a bedtime story but I wasn't listening. I had to listen for the threatening thump of a giant walking octopus with a human head. It had slaked out of the river behind the house and was now pounding down the path in the forest that was the extent of my known world. The thumping became so loud as the creature approached. Suddenly it was so close to the house that, like all nightmares, I had to wake up.

From the calm water behind C Island, I scanned the eastern shore for a wide channel. It would not be easy to spot from where I was, so I paddled blindly towards the shoreline. I didn't spot the channel until I was nearly on top of it. I had to toast the map's accuracy.

As I moved into the channel it narrowed and I found a mangrove island sporting a Mohawk haircut. The channel narrowed even further. The waters became quiet enough for me to notice my sprained back

157

muscles and that spirited me away to the mountains of Nepal.

*

A few months earlier but a world away, a friend and I were in the Himalayas trekking the Annapurna trail. It began as a two or three day trip but as we got further into the mountains they seduced us and we kept going until we were nearly half way through the Annapurna trail. So we decided to hike the whole thing. But were hiking it backwards. There's a reason to do it counterclockwise not clockwise as we were. The ascent to Thorong-La, a nearly eighteen thousand-foot pass, is done gradually over several days in order to acclimate to the altitude. But do the trail clockwise and you have to ascend from the village of Jharkot at eleven thousand five hundred-feet to the eighteen thousand-foot pass, an ascent of over six thousand feet in only twelve hours. Challenging even if beginning from sea level, but certainly not recommended over 10,000 feet where your risk of serious altitude sickness is exponentially magnified. But we made a go of it and had a delightful oxygen-deprived time surviving the ordeal by chewing on horseradish pills and decongestants. Up on Thorong-la, I sat in a yurt holding a watery hot chocolate that a Tibetan woman gave me and experienced the most delightful hallucinations. I asked a guy in a superman outfit to take our picture: my friend, our guide and me standing in front of a stupa festooned in prayer flags. Then we skipped down the trail that descended into a canyon all the while singing and chewing on oxygen sandwiches in a state of euphoria. In several days we reached Hongde where from a tiny airstrip on the edge of possibility we could fly back to Katmandu.

But that's not what happened.

When we arrived at Hongde, our porter argued with us over the payment and held my backpack hostage causing us to miss the plane. The next chance to fly out would be in three days, and only if the weather was good, the pilot had to see clearly in order to bank into the canyon and commit to an approach.

On Tuesday, after an idyllic day in the mountains, we returned to the village and noticed the crutch-wielding Royal Nepal Airlines ticket agent limping past the payer wheels calling out to us,

"No plane tomorrow, no plane tomorrow, next week, next week maybe."

We were ashen. My friend's visa expired in two days.

Within minutes we decided to hike out to the highway at Besisahar where we could catch a bus to Katmandu. Normally it was a four-day trek, but we thought we could do it in two by walking day and night. We could sleep later on the plane. It seemed like a good idea.

We left at sunset.

As the last light of dusk receded from the canyon, we saw what we were in for. Night in the Himalaya was a complete black-out. We only saw what our headlamps lit. Around midnight, the trail descended a rocky creek where the going was slick and slippery. Our headlamps, just above our eyes, caused an optical illusion that flattening out the contours of the rocks and boulders, we saw no shadows. The eventual accident happened on the edge of a precipice, I slipped, and only because my flailing left arm wedged between two rocks did I stay on the trail. But as I spun, my heavy backpack whipped around yanking the muscles between my back and shoulder blades. My headlamp flipped off my head and flew gracefully down the gorge until it -tap, ting, dinged on the rocks far below and vanished.

*

The memory replayed nearly every time I felt a stinging pain in my back and in my kayak on the west coast wilderness of Florida, I felt it again.

I heard a lonely osprey call and I turned my head. Out of the corner of my eye I spotted North River Chickee nestled in the crook of the small unremarkable island I had just passed. Had it not been for the birdcall waking me from my Himalayan daydream, I would have continued upriver wondering where the stupid chickee was.

I brought the kayak about feeling relieved. I had arrived for my break much sooner that I estimated. It was only 10:30 AM. And an early lunch meant I had time to heat a can. That meant chili (with aspirin).

The food bag and the water came out easy but the propane tanks were stored very deep between the seat and the hull in the middle of the boat. Frustrating on any day but today reaching this far tried my patience. Even when I stretched the length of my arm,

160

I could just get one finger on the tip of the tank. It took three painful attempts before I clamped two fingers and a thumb on the tip and yanked it out. (Sorry, sprained arms, aspirin's coming.)

Reaching for, picking at, yanking open, wrenching apart; your fingers became bruised being used as vice grips and tweezers; most of camping was about this. (Did I mention biting? There's a lot of biting Teeth double as scissors in the wild).

The chili was exceptional. Best can ever! I added a tin of oysters -the art school delicacy and I amused myself by reading the labels. The oysters had only 40% sodium. Adding the crackers, cheese and the chili, Lunch had the nutritional value of two days of salt. I was making myself into a salt sculpture from the inside out.

*

I paddled away from chickee and immediately got bored. The North River was wide, gray and offered little scenery. It was like paddling down an empty six-lane highway. I longed for the little winding creeks and aquariums. Then as if it heard my whining, the river opened up to an even wider five hundred foot channel. The uneven shorelines made it impractical to paddle close to the bank so I had to stay in the middle. So, I started to meditate.

Even in the doldrums I turned the hours of paddling into paddling meditation; one, two, one, two, right paddle, left paddle. This was something I intended, this was to be a meditation retreat after all, an opportunity to immerse myself in what I had learned about Zen.

At the end of a point, I passed two islands that offered a little relief then continued upstream to the mouth of "The Cutoff". It was so straight I wondered if it may have been dredged, though I didn't see the point, the two rivers met up less than a mile upstream.

Meanwhile, I could hear the echo of far off engines on the water. I was close enough to the marina at Flamingo that I thought I might see a few boats today.

To my relief, "The Cutoff" winnowed down and became very pretty. Bright green mangrove leaves fluttered in the light breeze. It was a fantastically beautiful day, sunny, quiet and serene. The kind of day you hope for when you decide to take a wilderness trip.

Leaning back, gazing into the blue sky above, space opened around me. In the silence, my senses stretched out over the landscape.

I watched the paddles traverse my field of vision, shiny, amber wood masterfully shaped. Sculptural. In "The Cutoff" I set aside looking for cuts and creeks and just gazed into the sky and watched the birds rise on the warm air. I recited passages from the Dharma and poems from enlightened people I learned about who spent their adult lives in solitude and meditation:

In every direction there are things you know and recognize.

Leave them.

Do not look for rest or relief.

Do not let consciousness dwell on the products of existence,

On things that come and go.

Passages like that could bring me to tears no matter where I happened to be but now paddling in the Everglades backwoods, I was overwhelmed. Here surrounded by an ancient, ancient ecosystem, the natural play of light repeated day after day for millennium; I was an insignificant speck, a blink of an eye in geologic time. Before me and after, this creek would continue doing its magic unconcerned whether I was here to see it or not.

Just before I entered the wilderness, I attended a Zen retreat held in a private home. I was given the koan of Hyakujo's fox to "practice with" for the ten-days of meditation. The koan was in the form of an old Chinese story. It goes like this:

Once when Hyakujo, the abbot, was delivering a series of lectures on Zen, an old man attended them, unseen by the monks. At the end of each talk the monks left and so did he. But one day he remained after the monks had gone and Hyakujo asked him: `Who are you?'

The old man replied: `I am not a human being, but I was a human being when the Kashapa Buddha preached in this world. I was a Zen master and an abbot of this monastery. One day one of my students asked me whether 'the enlightened man is subject to the law of

163

causation?' I answered him: 'The enlightened man is not subject to the law of causation.' For this answer evidencing a clinging to absoluteness I became a fox for five hundred rebirths, and I am still a fox. Will you save me from this condition with your Zen words and let me get out of a fox's body? Now may I ask you: 'Is the enlightened man subject to the law of causation?'

Hyakujo said: `The enlightened man is one with the law of causation.'

At the words of Hyakujo, the old man was enlightened. `I am emancipated,' he said, paying homage with a deep bow. `I am no more a fox, but I have to leave my body in my dwelling place behind this mountain. Please perform a funeral for the abbot I was.' and he disappeared.

The next day Hyakujo gave an order through the chief monk to prepare a funeral. `No one was sick in the infirmary,' wondered the monks. `What does our teacher mean to do?'
After dinner Hyakujo led the monks out and around the mountain. In a cave, with his staff he poked out the corpse of an old fox and then performed the ceremony of cremation.
That evening Hyakujo gave a talk to the monks and told this story about the law of causation.
Obaku, a student, upon hearing this story, asked Hyakujo: `I understand that a long time ago because a certain person gave a wrong Zen answer, he became a fox for five hundred rebirths. Now I want to ask: If some modern master is asked many questions, and he always gives the right answer, what will become of him?'

Hyakujo said: `You come here near me and I will tell you.'

Obaku went near Hyakujo and slapped the teacher's face with this hand, for he knew this was the answer his teacher intended to give him.

Hyakujo clapped his hands and laughed at the discernment. `I thought a Persian had a red beard,' he said, `and now I know a Persian who has a red beard!'

This story was not from a culture I grew up with and much of the references were odd and curious, and yet it resonated.
Hyakujo's story was deeply moving. Much more moving than merely a sweet, old Chinese story should have been.
Many times discovering the old stories from the east, I was cradled in a sense of familiarity and of home, even a sense of nostalgia. I missed a life I had never lived. I could only speculate that I was remembering a former life I didn't know anything about consciously, but still felt in my heart.

On the seventh night of that Zen retreat after the simple closing tea ceremony that concluded each day, I retired to my tent in the back yard. But before I got there, I saw something move near the edge of the property. It was big enough to be a dog and I wondered if a stray had gotten over the fence. It's head moved up and down. It acted differently than a dog. It was shy and it stood without any hint of running away. It acted like an animal that knew how to be invisible and waited for me to pass by unaware that it was near. Then without concern, it turned and disappeared into the shadows but not before I saw its big, bushy tail.

How could I be blamed for thinking I had seen Hyakujo's Fox? I didn't even know if foxes lived this far south or whether what I had seen was a dog. I never did find out what it was, but I did solve the koan. I solved it on the last day of the retreat and I like to think it was because of the phantom fox.

*

After a mile, "The Cutoff" poured into Robert's River, I could have made the turn in my sleep. I paddled on about a "Cutoff's" length (somewhere along the way I started equating distances to other lengths of creeks and channels) and found the Robert's River chickee hidden in a gap in the mangroves. Once again I could have easily missed it, the way it was so well tucked into the mangroves.

I stopped for to stretch my legs and study my map on the sunny deck.

The Robert's and Lane Rivers ran parallel each other like the two fingers of a peace sign. Between them lay a fascinating labyrinth of ponds and connecting creeks. I followed the squiggly lines this way and that looking for a passage to the Lane River. It was just like working a maze game in the back of a magazine.

I found two routes but the first involved seven small ponds. If I had not been nearly stranded in the mud pond of death this morning I might have given it a go but now as the sun was far along in the sky, I had no taste for adventure. If I found myself in another labyrinth to nowhere or battling my way out of a muddy shoal, I would probably lose my mind. And would have no one to blame but myself.

I decided on the kiddee short cut further down the Robert's.

Finding the entrance was easy enough since nothing happened on the Robert's River until a confluence on the left side. The channel lay hidden around a bend.

In five hundred feet, the channel turned left in a tight oxbow. I passed a creek on the right. There was another bend and a small creek on the left. Here the channel thinned to about twenty feet. I came to what looked like a wall of mangroves. I took out my red maker and dotted the map. I turned right and followed a smaller creek to another wall. I turned left and braided the mangrove roots then marked the spot with a red dot.

The winding route managed to turn half a mile into two.

My creek opened up to a lagoon. I followed the right bank around a half circle turn that led to another lagoon this one very shallow and obviously not possible to paddle in, I stayed along the deeper mangrove shore. I got back to a creek about ten feet wide that continued for four hundred feet then entered the top of a lagoon shaped like two lungs. I dotted the locale on the map. I could see mud lit by the sun so I stayed close to the east bank. Close enough to grab mangrove roots if I needed to. I felt vindicated in abandoning the longer route through the labyrinth that would have likely had mud to wrestle with.

I passed through one more lagoon and into a channel that brought me out to the big, wide Lane River. Ta Da! Nailed the kiddee path!

There were two solid mud banks good enough to stand on. I needed to refill my tea. I came alongside and got out.

I was so focused on the route I realized that I went through the labyrinth without seeing it at all.

But now, looking around, I fell into awe. The vastness overwhelmed me. I stood high enough on the bank to see over the scrubby mangroves. Behind me I could see the labyrinth I had just passed through and beyond to Robert's River. Looking ahead I could see down the Lane River to its mouth and the vast stretches of Whitewater Bay. Across the river, beyond the long south bank I could see occasional hammocks, the tree islands and farther, the cumulous clouds dappled over the Florida Bay.

I stood on one of the few patches of soil for miles in any direction and the Everglades reverberated with life, in green and blue, in mangroves and birds and fish, in alligators and snakes and bees and dragonflies. Every thing was moving, the water, the sky, the birds and insects. I could see the vast movement of the tides sliding off the Everglades. I stood on the very edge of past and future. A being steeped in the millennia of ancestors and here I was, me, at the end of the labyrinth having arrived at home.

Because there it was, that feeling, the feeling of being home, the feeling that had been absent ever since I had returned from the East.

I placed my hands on my chest and took a deep, reverent breath.

*

I started out on the Lane heading upriver, directly east. The wind caught my back and I held out my paddles like a sail happy with the way the day was turning out: I had just over a mile to go, I was not stuck in the mud behind Watson River Chickee, I had not gotten lost in the labyrinth, I still had a boat and paddles, and somehow I was feeling almost no back pain.

I came to an island in the middle of the river that marked the final half-mile of the day. There was not much to think about from here on, I took a cursory look at the map and made a mental note of one feature to pay attention to just before the chickee. When I arrived there, it couldn't have been more deceiving. It didn't look like the fork in the river the map indicated. Instead what I saw was a shallow pond that opened up on the left. The river turned immediately north and away from it without more than a peek. It all looked perfectly obvious where to go. I had passed a heap of these features in the labyrinths. However taking the obvious river channel left you in a closed bay. It was a dead end.

Studying the map's tiny lines, the Lane River actually entered, even disappeared into the lagoon then flowed out just beyond a point of mangroves where it became a river again. So instead of what looked like the right path, I paddled into the lagoon.

As I passed through, I scanned the pond. It was clogged by dead trees and in the center, a meadow of sawgrass. I had a visceral response to this shallow, brown pool and recognized the danger. The river appeared just behind a point of mangroves. It swirled around in an S shape and opened into Lane Bay. The chickee was in plain view less than one hundred feet ahead tucked into the north shore.

As I closed in on the dock, I noticed a red stuff sack hanging on the beam. But it wasn't a stuff sack. It was a long, red Everglades Rat Snake. It is relatively harmless and non-venomous though it's good to keep in mind that snakes do not brush their teeth and any wildlife bite was prone to infection and meant a trip to the clinic.

The snake slipped off into the mangroves as I approached and I guessed it was used to freeing up the chickee when guests arrived around this time.

*

Several years after my Wilderness Waterway journey, I paddled Lane and North Rivers again. But this time I took only a basic brochure map since I knew the area quite well and paddle the path easily without it.

But that's not what happened.

The wilderness permit list was as follows:

Day 1 Hell's Bay

Day 2 Lane Bay

Day 3 Robert's River

Day 4 North River

Day 5 Lane Bay

Day 6 Paddle home

On this trip I wanted to see what I could discover about the condition of the mind-as one gets lost. My intention was to put myself into difficult places where finding the way out was not easy and observe it if I could. Observe until I saw the moment when I realized I didn't have a clue where I was or how to get out and why that happened.

Notes from the sketchbook, February 2004:

The distance from Robert's River to North River was short.

With the extra time, I made an excursion beyond "the cutoff" to find a passage apparently possible according to the map. It turned out that it was not possible.

-North was a quiet chickee behind a small mangrove island that I discovered I could walk around on.

I pulled the kayak onto the deck and reached for something inside, the whole boat rolled off the chickee nearly taking me with it.

I heard dolphins but didn't see them. Mostly I watched the water, the details of the waves and colors, a window on the workings of the universe.

From the North River chickee to Lane River chickee was expected to be brisk, a straight paddle I intended to make quick work of: Up North River, across The Cutoff, down Robert's River and up the Lane. 3 turns, that's it.

But that's not how it turned out.

I had gotten past Robert's River Chickee in only forty-five minutes.

As I neared the confluence of the Robert's and Lane River, I had a choice of taking a cut through a maze of mangroves and creeks, it was only about 200 yards. I went in and came out on the Lane flawlessly. (I had done it before).

I headed up the Lane River east.

The Lane was a wide river and I enjoyed thinking of other things until, just as I was expecting at any moment to see the chickee, I saw something not expected: A remote weather lab of the type I had seen several times before throughout the Everglades and Big Cypress (there was one behind Gunboat Island in the Shark river), but I had never seen one here in Lane Bay.

The more I paddled, the more wrong everything looked. Every point and patch of mangrove was out of place according to my simple map.

After paddling into a completely ass-backwards pond with many small pods of mangroves, I turned back to figure out where I got lost.

First I went down the Lane to a fork where the river split and came back together (a diamond shaped island in the middle of the river). There was a possibility here I made a mistake and took a cut on one side of the island and that's where I got to and found the weather lab. I paddled all the way around the island. I made sure this squared up with the map.

"OK, I know I am here." I thought to myself and proceeded back up river to the chickee.

But no...ten minutes later here I was staring at the weather lab again and the lagoon with the pods of mangroves that shouldn't be there.

What could I have done wrong?

I poured over the map and came up with two new possibilities: I saw that one was the most likely: I saw on the map that I could have taken a fork in the river that led me to a group of ponds with no exit. I explored this possibility but came back to the fork I entered in. it would have been of no difference whether I made this mistake or not.

I had wasted forty-five minutes of the day.

I was getting disoriented and I was getting angry.

Everything was questioned. Could I have blundered early on in the labyrinth between North and Lane and somehow be in a different river or got turned around so much I re-entered the North River thinking it was the Lane River?

Now I was so pissed off for getting lost in the "easy" Lane River, and even though I was nearly certain that I was on the Lane, I hauled off and, against a strong headwind and returned to the mouth of the Lane River. There I could prove where I was because I saw the sign there reminding boaters that this was a manatee zone, dammit!

Half an hour later there was the big obvious MANATEE ZONE sign at the very obvious mouth of the terrifically obvious Lane River. I WAS on the Lane River! There was no doubt.

What was wrong with this picture? Could the park service have relocated the chickee and not updated the map? That would suck. I cursed the park service and then I cursed my idiotic plan to use a poorly drawn brochure map when I had fantastically detailed satellite maps sitting on the bookshelf at home.

With no other choice, I went paddling back up the Lane River. I covered distance quickly with the help of a strong tail wind. I stopped where I could marking every sure bend and point in the river. By now the map was smeared with red confirmation dots and an X at every single turn. This was now my third time on the same water and I was getting to know it very well. Which is another danger: "knowing" the wrong patch of water.

...And once again, I confirmed I had done everything correctly: I was at the diamond shaped island in the middle of the Lane. The day was now getting short and if I didn't find the chickee I would have to make camp somehow or spend the night in the kayak. Camp Humiliation.

So here I was having confirmed and confirmed and done everything right,

Until...

I had a moment of clarity and revelation. I stared at the map intently and focused on the spot near the end of the Lane River, where I should have found the chickee and there, just before the bay with the weather station, I now took notice of the shallow lagoon to the south (my right side). I was meant to enter it. I had ignored it every time because the channel to the left "seemed" to be the

*Lane River continuing on. Instead, the Lane River
entered the shallow lagoon, kept to the north shoreline
and then became a substantial channel on the left, its
big, its not hard to see or anything like that.*

BUT, (stay with me here)

*On the map (my poorly rendered brochure map), there
is a creek that seems to be a dead end. But it only seems
to be a dead end because, on the printed map, the words
"LANE RIVER" are printed right over the creek. Had that
printing not been there you could easily see the creek
actually continues around a point then in and out of the
lagoon. AHA- that's where my mistake was and that's
where I got lost, and repeatedly ended up in Weather
Lab Pond –the pond of disorientation.*

*

In the comfort of my living room couch, I analyzed that
day and focused on the actual look of the turn where I
got deceived.

The channel I thought was the Lane River flowed that
into to "Weather Lab Pond" had the strongest current,
so there probably was an exit somewhere. The first
time I had gone down the Lane River I had the good
map, I knew about the deceiving turn and didn't go to
Weather Lab Pond. So I had no memory of what going
there looked like.

I kept on repeating the mistake because:

1. I simply forgot.

2. I didn't know how far I was along the Lane River when I went into Weather   Lab Pond so I was not looking for the area that went into and out of the mud   lagoon.

But of course you don't know its there. Doubt washes away the mental map and you're lost in the labyrinth.

Finding the weather station had something to do with the disorientation. How could I have not thought I had taken another river? How could I have missed such an obvious landmark as the weather station on my first trip on the Lane?

The day after getting lost I took a paddle around Weather Lab Pond. I went to the spot where I turned back. I estimated it was less than five hundred feet through the mangrove from the chickee. I was that close. I also discovered that if I had pressed on, I would have found that the mangrove thinned and Lane Bay became visible, and, if I had understood at the time what I was looking at, I could have squeezed through a kayak-sized gap in what was no more than a mangrove hedge and paddle out about six meters. I would have seen the chickee on my right. In plain view a stone's throw away.

Later in the studio, I found my original highly detailed Wilderness Waterway maps. "LANE RIVER" was not printed over the critical turn. On the good map it was obvious which direction to go. What's more, Weather Station Bay was clearly identified as a closed bay. Even the kayak-sized gap was not shown (I'll bet it was dug by all the other paddlers finding themselves in Weather Station Bay just like me.)

I didn't take those maps along. The laminating had come loose and water would have soaked the paper. They would have been ruined. I felt they were an archive to be cared for as personal history (though when I was writing this manuscript they were nowhere to be found).

Had I known that using the simpler map would mean paddling the Lane River three times (at least once in panic and frustration as the sun was getting low) I would never had done it. But you don't know. No one has yet solved the problem of how to know, how to anticipate the unexpected.

Here was a perfect example of the disaster being determined long before you knew anything had gone wrong. The survivalist's "moment of no return" on the impossibly easy Lane River was the moment I packed the brochure map. And that was long before I got into the kayak.

*

The propane stove radiated a beautiful blue flame in the twilight. I prepared a breakfast buffet, oatmeal, apples, raisins, mandarin oranges, cashews crackers, peanut butter and Chinese tea.

The morning glow began purple then imperceptibly transitioned to brilliant gold. It filled the eastern sky above and reflected off Lane Bay before the sun rose washing the chickee in yellow light. I took a few photos of the spectacle hoping the slide film might record it.

I prepared my travel thermos of tea then poured the remaining two gallons of water out on the mangroves. Over the days I had become efficient in all my movements. I unpacked just what I needed, had the tent up and always had my lighting up before dark. In the morning I let things air out while I packed and prepared just enough food for the day. My routine arriving and departing became a dance and I'm sure the time spent making and breaking camp had been reduced by half since my first day. Each day my boat floated higher and lighter.

That said I had little or no time to draw or paint and I took very few photos. The problem was it took too long to extract the camera. I had to be careful to keep it dry. Disposable waterproof cameras were available at the time and I would have done very well having one or two bobbing in the kayak with me. A photo taken by a bad camera beats a photo not taken by a good camera any day.

*

In the time-protracted view of early morning, I paddled back down the Lane River passing Mud and Grass Lagoon, Diamond Island and the giant sign at the mouth that reminded boaters to slow down in manatee country.

The manatee population had dropped to less than one thousand when it was listed under the Marine Mammals Protection Act of 1973. New rules for boating speed in channels and rivers greatly reduced the possibility of impact and their numbers doubled. By the time I paddled the Wilderness Waterway twenty-seven years later, manatee sightings became more common. Today the manatee population is well over six thousand and this number is very likely too low. When a blast of cold air moved across the Florida peninsula recently, an aerial survey counted over 4,000 manatees in Tampa Bay alone. Due to conservation efforts we have many more sea turtles, many more alligators, more black bear and slowly we are recovering our crocodiles. The alligator was removed from the endangered species list. The black bear is rapidly heading that direction and the manatee possibly. The Florida Panther numbers have gone up as well but a shrinking rangeland for what is naturally a roaming predator are adding to the challenges for this wildcat. Eventually we may have to learn to live with panthers wandering our golf courses, parks and neighborhoods the same way we have gotten used to the alligator.

The intimate labyrinths were over, my last day would be in the windswept open water that characterized the ragged eastern shore of Whitewater Bay.

Out of the Lane River, I moved into a widening cone-shaped bay. Wind blew straight in from the Gulf and I got my first glimpse of whitecaps. The kayak bobbed about and triggered the memory of the creature that swam under it me back in "The Nightmare".

I could see calm waters behind the mangroves on the western shore of a long peninsula so I headed there. I had to keep my bow pointed into the waves to avoid getting quartered. I had hoped my final day on the water would be one of calm reflection but there was going to be none of that.

The windblown chop was annoying but once I got the kayak moving on the right course and found the right speed, she cut through both air and water, batting the chop aside and skipping over the whitecaps like a deftly tossed stone.

As I paddled in rhythm to crest and trough, a fine, satisfying spray came off the bow and in no time at all I was entering the calm on the east shore.

As I slid near the mangroves, a giant plume of whitewater exploded off the bow like a bomb. My boat lifted up to an impossible height and then came down with a backbreaking thud. The water turned brown with mud.

I came about. I saw a moving line of muddy water like a jet's contrail running from my kayak out to the bay.

"A manatee, an alligator or a crocodile? What was it? The first two were no problem but the latter would be trouble. I didn't like the idea of paddling this bay knowing there were crocs hidden in it, including the crocodile I just spooked the hell out of.

I moved on quickly. It had to be a manatee, I decided. The mud trail went straight out, and the blooms of mud in the deeper water indicated the up and down flapping of a fluke and not the snakelike swish of a reptile. Still it was strong enough to lift the boat up out of the water. Big things even if they are considered docile are still dangerous. A cow can kill you if it falls on you. (I've had fights with cows, in France, but that's another story).

I paddled along a shoreline littered with logs and branches as imposing as barbed wire. They all pointed in one direction, another telltale sign of hurricane, probably the same one that gave Harney Creek chickee its cartoon tilt.

Hurricanes and the tornadoes they calve have left a record in the forests and swamps of Florida. I took a trip down the Peace River a few months after a hurricane struck the area and found a stretch of flattened trees all pointing north west. It looked like a landing field in the jungle. A tornado had obviously touched down and mowed down a few acres before disappearing. Within a year, the heaps of dry branches would fuel numerous wildfires, the second stage of destruction.

I came to the end of the east bank where just a wisp of stunted mangroves held on. I pointed the kayak downwind toward a channel barely visible on the opposite bank, just a shadow in the thin line of mangroves on the horizon.

I crossed rapidly with the wind and the shadow became a lagoon that coned down to a channel. The wind pushed me in behind the mangroves. The kayak surfed a wave from Whitewater Bay into flat calm. I had to think this was the daily routine of Whitewater Bay; calm at night with wind picking up by 10 AM as the sun heats the air until the afternoon when, I suppose like everything else, the wind takes a nap.

I passed through the channel and entered another big bay, the last of two big waters I would have to navigate. Ahead was an island. I took the map out from under my seat to double check my location and nearly lost it to a rogue gust of wind. I firmed up my plan and stowed the map deep under the seat. If I paddled the east shoreline of the island, I'd be in relatively calm waters to the very end of the point where I could cross with the wind again on my back.

*

My life at this time was a mixed bag, I had just sold my first seascape painting, a 40x60" oil on canvas. It sold for 10,000 dollars to a young Russian living in New York. Our gallery assistant, Nadia, sold it on New Year's Eve. Pierre, my business partner in the gallery, had gone to France quietly (permanently, I found out later) leaving me with the studios, nearly two thousand, five hundred sq ft of South Beach real estate to work with. But the noise and smoke from the nightclub below went on all night long. I would have traded it all in for a good night's sleep.

I sometimes thought the incentive for these expeditions had less to do with the wonders of nature and more to do with getting eight hours of good sleep.

*

I paddled to the point where the winds tugged at the stunted mangrove branches. I backed into a patch of hard mud to hold me on the shore while I refilled my tea mug. I double-checked that everything was tied down, even the flip-flops.

From my position, I could see the southwest shore was taking the full brunt of Whitewater's winds. The trees looked like seaweed swishing in a river current, waves

182

splashed on the bank cluttered by a nest of dead trees. It looked like trouble.

I took another look at the map. There was a needle-thin island east of me. It was half a mile paddle directly into the wind but the kayak did well and it would cut off two miles exposed to the broadside winds of Whitewater Bay.

I stowed my gear, tied a line to my paddle then pushed off the end of the point. I came about in the wind and started the crossing to Needle Thin Island. Whitecaps splashed on the bow. Instead of struggling the kayak again took to the headwind like a dolphin, my paddle dug into water and I felt the satisfying slide as the boat skipped on the waves. It was an excitement I hadn't had much of on this trip. It was a thrill! I made the half-mile crossing in no time. At the edge of Needle Thin Island I could see the calm water. As I approached I noticed no wind one foot above the water then two feet above. As I got closer to Needle Thin Island the wind was two and a half feet above the water and that was all I got. My face was in the wind but there was calm from my shoulders down. Bizarre.

I dug around in my seat pocket for something to plug my ears with. Wind is painful to the ears.

It was approaching 10 AM and the sound of powerboats crossing the bay became more frequent. The sports fishing fleet was just making its way out of the channel to Coot Bay. My time on the water was whittling down to its last few hours. The harbormaster (who had my car keys) would be there no later than five PM, it was the first deadline of the trip besides the deadline I always had: nightfall and tide.

Needle Thin Island came to an end. Time to make the crossing to the windswept south shore of Whitewater Bay. I took sight of a feature, a point on the tip of a bight maybe half a mile away (half of Avocado Creek). I would head for that point and see what happens.

By now all the calories from breakfast were used up and the caffeine had only a cursory effect. My stomach protested but a place for lunch was far off.

I set my sights on a picnic along Coot Bay at a trailhead to Mud Lake.

It was a well-established trail complete with a dock and signage, a perfect destination for the semi-hearty day-tripper renting canoes out of Flamingo. Though on a blustery day such as this, my guess was the average sunny day paddler looking at the winds and white caps of Coot Bay would have scurried back to the car.

I took just such a novice day trip with my fellow artist Frederic five years ago. We later referred to it as the "bloodsucker tour".

It was August, high season for mosquitoes and as soon as we parked at Flamingo Marina, I felt the first tingling stings on my arms and neck. But we were motivated and went ahead with renting a canoe. We nearly slapped ourselves silly attempting to paddle away from the launch.

After about twenty feet of adventure, we returned to the outfitter store where Frederic and I bought full-length mosquito suits for fifty dollars each.

I remember thinking Frederic looking like a man in a gray cloud of smoke. I suppose I looked the same. We returned to the canoe and paddled into the middle of the canal. Then we stopped to marvel at the squadron of mosquitoes unsuccessfully trying to get at our skin.

We paddled the two-mile long dredged channel to Coot Bay and tied up at the Mud Lake Canoe Trail dock. It was a dark mangrove-covered walking path actually, presumably a portage.

As we walked, the trail got darker and darker. It seemed like the day had become cloudy. In five hundred feet we came to a dredged creek sized channel with scarcely enough water for a frog, let alone a canoe. Mangroves branches reached over it in all directions. I bent down to see how far the creek went. It disappeared into the gathering darkness.

"Maybe it's going to rain," Frederick said.

I stood up and things got brighter. And then they got darker. My eyes focused on the dark fuzzy spots an inch or two from my face.

Hundreds of mosquitoes orbited my head. Hundreds more crawled on the netting, their tiny stingers stabbing away through the gaps trying to connect with skin.

"Noooo, it's the mosquitoes! We're in a cloud of mosquitoes! Ruuuuuuun!"

And we did run.

We turned and ran like cartoons away from a cartoon bomb that had dropped at our feet.

The forest became significantly brighter as the bugs blew off of our netting. We jumped into the canoe and paddled far out into the middle of Coot Bay. Mosquitoes covered the aluminum interior of the canoe and we swatted and them with our life vests leaving black stains on the aluminum hull.

The mosquitoes thinned out.

"They can drain all your blood," Frederic said.

"Death by mosquito," I said.

A warm shower started falling. Since I had brought it along, I opened an umbrella. I watched the raindrops make tiny circles in the glasslike water. The bay was utterly motionless. The world became serene under the umbrella.

"The mosquitoes had covered my head net. They blocked out the light."

"Yes. They crowded together to cut off my oxygen," Frederick observed, "I couldn't breath. They are very smart."

A powerboat came to a stop nearby. A man cast his line. He looked at us with disdain, a look that said 'you are an insult to everyone on the water'.

"Expecting rain?" he asked sarcastically.

186

We must have looked like a couple of stupid day tourists, the kind of duffers this guy probably had seen enough of.

Now, in the winds on the tip of Needle Thin Island, saturated in brackish, briny water and sweat, I had become a well-seasoned backwoodsman and would command the respect of anyone on the water. After eleven days of paddling I could look at a day fishermen like that fellow and produce such a smirk as to put his tail between his legs and make him scurry home to momma.

I pushed off the point and let the wind blow me to the west shore spouting a pirate's *"Arrrrrrr"* to close the deal.

*

I am not one for guidebooks. They may be useful for a day or two but the big problem with them is that everyone has the same guidebook and is following it toe to toe. If you've arrived in a picturesque village and go to a restaurant suggested in the book, you'll find the same people you saw on Gili Island asking for the guidebook recommended ceviche or coconut pie. They are dressed in the same yoga slacks they bought in Nepal a thousand miles away at a store mentioned in one short sentence in the guidebook. This effect will eventually turn you misanthropically insane.

If you were to follow the Wilderness Waterway guidebook, it recommends paddling from Shark River chickee down the Shark River, turning into the Shark Cutoff then navigating a series of wide and winding channels to Oyster Bay where you embarked on a windy, wavy paddle straight down the middle of the massive two-mile wide Whitewater Bay -*for it's entire length of six miles*, an insane suggestion and a dangerous one! I would have no interest in finishing my one hundred-mile long trip with that.

Once I got off the habit of using guidebooks I did much better. I started to learn the local dialect and politics and sometimes wandered in neighborhoods where people actually went about their business and wouldn't mind giving you a humbling dose of what they really thought of your see-the-world privilege.

*

As I approached the bight, I saw it had the shape of a manta ray's mouth complete with the two oar-like lips on either side. If I adjusted my course toward the western point of Manta Ray Bight, I could bypass the open mouth altogether.

But as I turned ever so slightly, just a matter of degrees really, the waves slapped the stern half-broadside and caused a formidable wobble. It was like a bull kicking the tail of the kayak, the difference was striking. If I were in a canoe, I would have flipped it. I kept the kayak pointed and with some trail and error, I learned to lean into the crest with my right paddle and then lean over my paddle on the left side as I fell into the trough. Then I could ride the waves quite well, and every fifth or sixth wave I could even surf down a crest. But I had to concentrate. This wave pattern felt like standing still on a wobbling tightrope.

The west lip of Manta Ray Bight was not an inviting place. Like most of Whitewater Bay, the shore was just a pile of white mangrove skeletons in shallow mud where brown sea foam blew in the wind.

I had to come-about and tack several times to keep from slamming into the prickly shoreline. All the while I pined for the hidden creeks, ponds and the intimate silence of the labyrinths.

I took my last tack and Whitewater Bay funneled into Tarpon Creek. I surfed the last wave into calm water behind the mangroves like I was shot out the end of a waterslide. The wind vanished. I stopped paddling and had a little celebration. Phew! Whitewater was over.

Tarpon Creek carried on for half a mile. It turned left then right and opened up to Coot Bay. I felt a tingle of euphoria knowing perhaps that this was the last bay of the journey.

A powerboat passed nearby without putting out a wake. I was getting close to the marina. On the other side of Coot Bay, I could see the flashing silver reflection of canoes, the dull thud of day-trippers banging paddles clumsily against the hull.

I hugged the west shore not to avoid wind but because it looked wild and familiar. It looked like a friend.

It was just before noon when I tied up at the dock of Mud Lake Canoe Trail to have lunch on the picnic bench. None of the clumsy canoes had made it here and with the wind blowing like it was, I expected none would bother.

Afterward lunch I walked the foot trail to Mud Lake. On this sunny winter day, there were virtually no mosquitoes.

As before, the shallow canoe trail was just a spit and yet it was clearly marked on the map as a day trip.

The canopy of trees opened to the sky and on first sight I had a better name for Mud Lake: Mud and Gator Lake. Six alligators basked in the sun right nearby the trailhead. To me, this place was obviously a muddy death trap. A shiver went down my spine surveying the brown pudding. How could this chocolate mousse be recommended as a day trip? I imagined an inexperienced paddler taking their first knee-deep step into that mud to pull the canoe to shore. It would have been a long wait with the alligators before help came. I decided the word "canoe" should be removed and this trail renamed "Mud Lake Walking Trail".

Then I hatched a multiple-choice question,

"What's more dangerous to a kayaker?"

1 Mud

2 A lot of mud

3 A lake of mud

Answer: All of the above.

As I walked back, I could hear the whine of boat engines echo through the forest. The mid-day sport fishing rush was on. I gave the picnic site a thorough cleaning, slipped into my kayak with the grace of a dancer and paddled on. With every stroke I seemed to become more aware of the sunlight, the blue shimmer of the water, the splash and the drip of the paddles, felt the air on my skin and saw the light and shadow play in the mangroves. I could feel the vibration of a living, moving planet.

I passed the tip of the bight of Coot Bay and spotted the access canal to Flamingo Marina and the Florida Bay.

I was home free. I didn't scrape a hole in the hull the first morning. I didn't sink in Chokoloskee Bay. I didn't get hopelessly lost in the labyrinths. I did not get stranded in the mud behind Watson River chickee (where no one would have found my bleached bones). All these scenarios seemed like exaggerated stories to me now, but at the moment I would have given them even odds.

I leaned back and paddled my kayak like the expert I had become. I put my feet up and silently scooped at the still and shimmering canal, my paddles barely disturbing the water. People in canoes passed by (I heard them banging their aluminum and plastic paddles against the rental canoes long before I saw them). I slipped by some without being noticed. I could easily imagine natives of the New World magically becoming invisible to the first European explorers in this way. Silence is a form of invisibility. And I had become as silent and still as a forest pool.

The kayak retreat had immersed me in the very DNA of the Everglades.

I paddled along the high shoreline of the canal's oolitic rock, the exposed limestone sediment of an ancient sea from a time when there was no ice on the poles of the Earth and the sea was two hundred feet higher and Antarctica was covered in tropical ferns.

From the sketchbook, South East Asia:

In the theatre of time,

The white curtains rise.

She lay there on the beach,

Her head on a sand pillow

I made for her.

In my hand,

The fossil of an ancient horse

That cantered this very landscape

30,000 years earlier.

A procreate.

An orphan.

A child.

Whispering of

Wealth and brevity.

Before we began,

I watched the

Pristine sea shimmer,

Immaculate.

Immaculate.

Then: a gesture from backstage.

A discernable distinction

Between stillness and stirring.

Raindrops skittered on the pregnant swells.

Spreading wind, wings and water.

And with no thoughts for 10,000 miles,

With no one to hear the tiny "c" note,

No one to taste the salty quiver,

No one to feel the breeze cup the face,

No one to see the stone fish leap,

With no one to smell the aroma of

Marl and bones,

What else were we to do

But hide ourselves

In each and every thing.

The day-trippers wanted to talk to me as I passed by.

The conversations were short:

"How long you going out for?"

"I've been out 12 days"

"Wow!"

Or:

"How long ya' been out for?"

I've been out 12 days."

"Wow!"

Or:

"How far to the Mud Lake Canoe Trail?"

"Don't go. Unless you want to get stuck in the mud overnight."

"Wow!"

Or:

"How far to Coot Bay?"

"How fast are you going?"

"Wow!"

And on and on and on, no one seemed to care what I answered.

I heard one man say,

"That guy knows what he's doing."

True. I did know what I was doing.

I gave him a smile and a wave. It was easier to do, I hadn't used my voice since Canepatch and even then for only about 20 minutes of hushed banter, now I was nearly yelling responses. My vocal cords had withered from the lack of use. It made me sound like a whining, sick child. I pushed my voice further and then sounded like a yodeler.

Just as difficult was listening. Everyone seemed to have adopted a southern drawl as if they lived on an Alabama chicken farm their whole life.

And the banter was so excessive and egocentric, trying to sound smart, or smarter than the next guy. They used words like a spear, like a weapon. I didn't like the sound of it and I didn't look forward to chatting up strangers at the marina.

I recalled the meditation retreats in Thailand: one hundred or more students passing the day sitting

together with only the sound of bells and chanting.
Now I really understood the purpose of silence in
spiritual practice.

The 12-day trip may have been worth it for that
insight alone.

A good deal of powerboats were passing by now and
they didn't bother with the no-wake rules. My kayak
bobbed up and down but I didn't care. I was at the end
of the journey and I was in the most amazingly soft
ecstasy. A cool, peaceful spring of insight babbled in
my mind. My paddle: the staff of a sage.

From the sketchbook

Wat Suan Mokkh Monastery, Thailand.

We saw him earlier,

In the thicket near where Cobra lives.

But now we could not find him.

He had become a disappeared one.

Sitting cross-legged by the heliconias and jasmine.

Sitting, with no ear to hear our footsteps,

No eyes to see our dusky, dim form,

*We knew there was no way we were going to be greeted
then.*

Slowly,

We circumnavigated the seamless pagoda he left behind.

Though, try as I might, I could not find and end to it.

Whispering,

Maybe,

Or calling

While the clouds passed,

I heard the

Drip, drip, drip

Of rain trickling off the pagoda's roof.

You had sung the marigold's chime,

There by the roadside,

Before there was radio,

Before telephone,

Where the men gathered to settle a negotiated boundary.

This morning, I saw Cobra sliding through the grass in the coconut grove,

There was nothing left to do but watch her.

And I wondered aloud.

Did she, too, see the Earth below her become fathomless-ly transparent.

Did she, too, see the mountain spit trees that grew and died in the blink of

Cobra's monacled eye.

Did she, too, see so-called life and death as wave after wave uninterrupted.

You too, old Buddhadasa, you saw it in the sanskrit, didn't you?

"No re-birth" you said.

And although they wouldn't accept it,

Cobra knew.

Cobra knew, too, of uncertainty and doubt before a journey.

Though she may never leave her forest.

She saw in the blink of a monacled eye,

The magic circus

Flatten and disperse in the combing forest wind.

Cobra stood on her long neck to sense the air.

She stood in the middle of her forest.

A world of hanging vines and green hot ponds.

A half-moon lassoed by a night rainbow as her
established nimitta.

Then in the gathered silence,

Not moving,

Barely breathing,

We saw him, clear and obvious:

The Disappeared One

In the gap between past

And what is yet to come.

*

A bridge appeared over the canal. A bridge!

I watched with eye-popping wonder as a car hissed across in a blur of silver.

It was the main park road, state highway 9336. I lowered my paddles and let the current take me under the moss-covered concrete. Trickling sounds of the boat echoed off the ceiling. And soon after I passed under, the trees subsided and sunlight filled the canal. In ten minutes I arrived at Flamingo Marina. I gawked at the manufactured landscape, the flat acreage of grass, the armada of aluminum boat trailers lined up in the parking lot and the coral-colored out buildings. The morning rush was apparently over and but for a few people milling about the store, the place looked deserted.

The canal abruptly ended at a metal dam that looked like the gray riveted side of a battleship. In front, an American Crocodile sunbathed in a shallow pool. In Yellowstone, we called them *"the company bear"* the animals that seemed to stand by the road just for tourists to photograph as if placed there by the staff.

I hauled the kayak out of the water and pulled it away from the slip. The whispering hisssss it made as it slid across the warm grass made me smile. Warm, dry grass! I just wanted to lie down on it and have long nap.

At the far end of the parking lot I recognized my truck. I walked over to the harbormaster station. He was an older man, the years spent on a boat showed in his craggy, sun-dried skin. He reminded me of Rod Steiger in the film version of Ray Bradbury's *The Illustrated Man*. I appreciated how he edited his words.

"You're the silver Cherokee?"

"Yep." I said.

He took my keys off a corkboard festooned with rows of hardware store hooks and handed them to me, "He'y go,"

He didn't ask how my trip was. He didn't need to. He could see it on my face. And in our brief exchange, I knew he'd seen that look before.

He could see the dolphins plying the morning pond and taste the fragrant, cool air at dawn.

He saw Avocado Creek and Canepatch, and the meditation cushion under the banana leaves. He saw the golden paddle and the arc of diamonds cascading from the blade, the bees buzzing on the wild blossoms, the splash of the manatee's fluke, the cloud rolling in a lazy, lazy blue sky.

Standing free on a mound of soil gazing over the vast horizon from the south tip of the continent witness to all the workings of time in the world, there was no need to ask how my trip was.

My struggle, my search for home was fundamentally a search for the self. But the self is fluid and changes constantly with the surroundings. A fact that always seems to confound us.

In the 11th century, Japanese Zen master Dogen wrote:

To study the self is to forget the self.
To forget the self is to become intimate with the ten thousand things.
To become intimate, body and mind drop away.
No trace of enlightenment remains, and this no-trace continues endlessly.

I saw the face of the labyrinth, the ten thousand things, the endless choices, the possibilities and dangers. The silent teacher, the prodding mother, the Zen master, they were all watching and waiting for the student to see not the finger pointing, but where the finger points.

In his time Dogen was considered a revolutionary monk, a threat to the dynasty and so lived in exile in a monastery deep in a mountainous wilderness and yet his intimate words separated by the centuries spoke directly to my heart.

The old man, the Buddha, the old radical, preached the ultimate prescription to the conundrum of existence. In India at that time, becoming a monk meant becoming homeless and wandering the world living in the forest or in barns accepting what was freely given and devoting the days to meditation.

I brought the truck around and stood for a while just looking at the kayak and all the gear spread out on the grass. I picked up my paddles. I felt the stability and strength and admired the varnish sparkling in the sun. I snapped them apart as a passage from the Diamond Sutra came to mind, a Sutra that spoke of the wonder and love of the world that comes from being no one and nowhere. Of a self that is free and fluid and dancing in the world of forms,

Thus shall you think of this fleeting world:
A star at dawn,

A bubble in a stream;

A flash of lightning in a summer cloud;

A flickering lamp,

A phantom,

And a dream.

~Mark Rutkowski, Miami Beach, 2017

Made in the USA
Middletown, DE
24 November 2017